WILL
PLANET
EARTH
BE
DESTROYED?

WILLIAM BELL

But the day of the Lord will come as a thief in the night, in which the heavens will pass away with a great noise, and the elements will melt with fervent heat; both the earth and the works that are in it will be burned up."

For behold, I create new heavens and a new earth; And the former shall not be remembered or come to mind. But be glad in what I create; For behold I create Jerusalem as a rejoicing, and her people a joy.

3 Peter 3:10; Isaiah 65:17-18

Table of Contents

Introduction

Will Planet Earth Be Destroyed? For many, the study of the end times, i.e. the coming of Christ and the end of the world means the destruction of the planet. Most who study the Bible believe this view is taught in the Scriptures. I can also remember when this was my belief. However, I gained a more accurate understanding of God's word by ignoring most of my "learned professors" and by learning to do my own Bible research with the aid of a few honest men.

I continue the journey of growth and discovery in the area of end times research. God's word often challenges me to do further research, double and triple check a text that I thought I was familiar with, only to learn or see some angle which I hadn't noticed before. Yet, it was there all the time. It required hours of careful reflection and consulting with the works of those who are my peers and others who have a greater depth of scholarship than I have time to acquire. Their knowledge and skill is of immense help in the disciplines of word studies and history.

For many, the end of the world is a frightening subject. I remember about 40 years ago, when my youngest daughter, my wife and I were playing in our back yard. We heard a loud explosion. Looking up in the air we saw ball of fire. My daughter immediately began to cry. My first thought was the world is ending. Then after looking more closely, I discovered that two planes, one small aircraft and a jet had collided in mid-air not far from our house. People have all sorts of events they believe are the end to the world. The release of the movie 2012, caused even more focus on the end times following the very successful "Left Behind series by Tim LaHaye and Jerry Jenkins. Some have called suicide lines to get help because they fear having to suffer through events like the ones shown in those movies.

We want you to lay those fears aside. While this is more of an exegetical study, and not a fictional feel good book, if you understand what's written here, you will feel relieved knowing that you don't have to fear a cataclysmic destruction of the world. You'll be able to walk in confidence and peace, knowing the love of God and his promises to provide for you every day of your life through his wonderful creation. You will feel blessed and assured that God's promise to maintain his creation is sure and steadfast.

In this study, you will learn how to interpret the meaning of many passages believed by some to speak about the end of planet earth. You will learn that these passages do not teach a coming destruction of the universe at all. Some concepts and ideas from Scripture may be unfamiliar at first, but in time, you will come to see how transparently clear and simple the Bible is on this matter of end times prophecy.

We'll survey some passages in both the Old and New Testaments. Grab a pen and paper to write down any questions you may have. Make notes of the Scriptures you'd like to discuss further. You may email those questions to me at info@allthingsfulfilled.com.

Also, I critiqued Ted J. Clarke's view where he attempts to prove a future global judgment. His arguments were valuable in helping to clarify certain nuances of the subject. It's always good to test your ideas and conclusions through those who have opposing views. As a kite rises against the wind, truth shines brighter against the backdrop of error.

The views expressed here are my own and even where ideas are borrowed no one is to be held responsible for the manner in which I've used them. Our chief concern here is the study of the subject of the end of planet earth as used in Bible prophecy. Does it mean the entire planet or even universe or does it mean a local region as applied in end times prophecy? That's the question we seek to answer.

Chapter 1:
Definition of Terms

The use of the term "earth" in the Bible particularly in the destruction of the world (de-creation) texts is from the Hebrew word "eretz". *Beyond Creation Science* (BCS) documents that eretz carries no inherent global or spherical connotation in Hebrew.

Eretz is translated as land in the Old Testament over a thousand times. It is also repeatedly translated as "country" and "ground." The majority usage of eretz in the Old Testament refers to a local region of land.[1]

Martin and Vaughn also quoted conservative Hebrew scholar, Gleason Archer who explained one of the textual problems in the use of eretz particularly in Genesis 7. "In explanation of this assertion [that the flood was local, not global] it needs to be pointed out that the Hebrew 'eretz', translated consistently as "earth" in our English Bibles, is also the word for "land" (e.g. the land of Israel, the land of Egypt). There is another term, *tebel,* which means the whole expanse of the earth as a whole. Nowhere does *tebe*l occur in this account, but only *'eretz',* in all the statements that sound quite universal in the English Bible.

While we appreciate the attention and dialogue BCS brings to the discussion of eschatology, it should be noted that there are some issues with seeing the flood as local. For instance, in Genesis 8:21, God said he would never destroy all living things as he had done. If the flood were merely a local event, then would God not be saying that he would never again bring a local flood?

---

[1] Timothy P. Martin and Jeffrey L. Vaughn, Beyond Creation Science, Covenant Creation from Genesis to Revelation, c. p. 130.

Secondly, though an event may be geographically confined to a local area that by no means suggests that it did not have a universal scope or impact. Jesus died outside the gates of Jerusalem, but his death influences the entire globe. Its impact even reached back to creation, affected both heaven and earth, and even extended to the depths of Sheol (Hades), i.e. beneath the grave. (See Matthew 23:32-37 and 24:30; 26:63-64.

Examples of the Use in the Old Testament

Genesis 12:1

Now the Lord had said to Abram: Get out of your country [*eretz, earth*] from your family and from your father's house, to a land [*eretz, earth*] I will show you. Abraham was called to leave the *eretz*. That is the word translated as earth. It shows that earth is used to speak of less than the globe. Abraham was not called upon to leave the planet and go to another planet or galaxy.

Ezra 1:2

"Thus says Cyrus king of Persia: All the kingdoms of the earth the Lord God of Heaven has given me. And He has commanded me to build Him a house at Jerusalem which is Judah."

We must ask here, was Cyrus' kingdom a global kingdom? Historical records demonstrate to the contrary. This text speaks of the regional area over which Cyrus ruled.

Habakkuk 1:6

"For indeed I am raising up the Chaldeans, a bitter and hasty nation which marches through the breadth of the earth, to possess dwelling places that are not theirs."

What about the territory of the Babylonians? Did they conquer the entire globe? Babylon ruled the world of their day but there is no evidence that their kingdom included the entire globe. The Greek equivalent to the Hebrew word eretz is ge. The apostles understood and used the term "ge" in the same manner in which the Hebrew word eretz was used. They quote from the Septuagint (LXX) version of the Bible that translated *eretz* as *ge* in the New Testament. It is clear that Jesus used the word ge (earth) to represent the land of Palestine.

"Then the sign of the Son of Man will appear in heaven, and then all the tribes of the earth will mourn, and they will see the Son of Man coming on the clouds of heaven with power and great glory." (Matt. 24:30) This verse is equivalent to Revelation 1:7, both of which are quotes in part from Zechariah 12:10-12. The tribes of the land refer primarily to those of the house of David.

That means Jesus is referring to the Southern kingdom of Israel. The most generous of applications would only include the entire 12 tribes of Israel. Thus, the earth as used in the text is regional and not global. That this text refers to the fall of Jerusalem in AD70 is clear from Jesus' words which state His generation would not pass until all were fulfilled, Matt. 24:34.

Genesis 11:8,9

That γης (ges) is not limited to the land of Palestine or to any particular local geographical area is evident from other texts. At the tower of Babel, just a few years removed from the flood, Genesis records that men were scattered all over the face of the earth (eretz). "So the Lord scattered them abroad from there over the face of all the earth, and they ceased building the city. Therefore its name is called Babel, because there the Lord confused the language of all the earth; and from there the LORD scattered them abroad over the face of all the earth.

Matthew 4:8 and Luke 4:6

Satan tempts the Lord by offering him all the kingdoms of the world. While the term eretz is not used, one would be hard-pressed to deny that there was no land (eretz) in these kingdoms. The very word kingdom derives from king and "dom" short for "domain" (land or territory).

Acts 17:26

"And He has made from one blood every nation of men to dwell on all the face of the earth, and has determined their preappointed times and the boundaries of their dwellings." It would be irresponsible to claim that every nation dwelled in one local area or even on one continent.

Chapter 2:
Jesus, Moses and the Prophets

The Prophet's taught and applied the Law of Moses to the people of Israel. Jesus expressed it in this manner. "Do not think that I came to destroy the Law or the Prophets. I did not come to destroy but to fulfill. For assuredly, I say to you, till heaven and earth pass away, one jot or one tittle will by no means pass from the law till all is fulfilled," (Matt. 5:17-18).

Jesus' words demand that he did not bring a different message than Moses. Observe the eschatological tone of the words, marked by "till heaven and earth pass,' and "till all is fulfilled." Thus, Jesus addressed the end time prophecies in his statement to include the passing of heaven and earth. He saw the fulfillment of the law and the prophets as the time of fulfillment of every jot and tittle of Old Covenant prophecy.

Peter and Paul taught from the Law and the Prophets as their source of end times prophecy. What is important to note here is that we have the Lord, the apostle to the Jews, and the apostle to the Gentiles all saying they preached one message. See also 1 Cor. 15:11, Gal. 1:8, 9, 2 Pet. 2:2.

Peter, Moses and the Prophets, Acts 3:24-26

For Moses truly said to the fathers, 'The Lord your God will raise up for you a Prophet like me from your brethren. Him you shall hear in all things, whatever he says to you. And it shall be that every soul who will not hear that Prophet shall be utterly destroyed from among the people. Yes, and all the prophets, from Samuel and those who follow, as many as have spoken, have also foretold these days," (Acts

3:22-24). Peter began with Moses then concluded with Samuel and all the Prophets.

Paul, Moses and the Prophets, Acts 26:22-23

Paul expressed the same in the following before Felix, the governor of Caesarea:

"But this I confess to you that according to the Way which they call a sect, so I worship the God of my fathers, believing all things which are written in the Law and in the Prophets. I have hope in God, which they themselves also accept, that there will [is about to, Mello] be a resurrection of the dead, both of the just and the unjust." (Acts 24:14-15) Therefore, having obtained help from God, to this day I stand, witnessing both to small and great, saying no other things than those which the Prophets and Moses said would come—that the Christ would suffer, and that He would be the first to rise from the dead, and would proclaim light to the Jewish people and to the Gentiles."

In these passages, Paul covers the scope of the gospel to include Jesus' death and resurrection, the preaching to both Jew and Gentile and the resurrection of the dead. The expression, "saying no other things than those which the Prophets and Moses said would come," pinpoints the focus and origin of his message. Not once did he veer off that divine model.

Having identified the source for Christ and the apostolic ministry, we now address two prophetic passages, which speak of burning the earth (eretz) with fire.

The Greek Word Mello

Citing Don K. Preston, who affirmed that the primary meaning of 'mello' with the [present] infinitive is 'about to be, to be on the point of' per Gross 4. Drew Leonard stated we promote mello because of texts such as Acts 17:31, Romans 8:18 and others because we want certain resurrection texts to be spoken of as imminent. Feeling the force of the argument as strengthening the A.D. 70 position, he cites an argument from Curtis Cates who commented on Acts 26:22-23 and

Romans 5:14. He accepts Cates argument that these texts pointed to an extremely distant event.

Cates asks the question "Does *mello* always mean 'to be about to be'? He answered No! We respond that there is not a Preterist we've ever met who says that it does. That's never been our argument. We have argued that "mello" with the **present infinitive** means "about to be", i.e. something imminent. Nor do we attempt to prove it on the basis of grammar and linguistics alone, but by allowing Scripture to interpret Scripture. Cates challenged Paul's statement in Acts 24:15, saying King wanted to leave the impression that the "resurrection both of the just and unjust" had to happen almost immediately.[2]

Widespread Inconsistency in Translation of Mello

There is no consistency in the translation of mello from one translation to another. Mello occurs 111 times in the NT. The percentage of times it is translated as imminent varies from a single time by the Wycliffe translation to a maximum of 108 times by the Kingdom Inter-linear Translation. Of those 111 times mello occurs in the New Testament, 50 of those references relate to eschatology. The number of times mello is translated to mean "imminent" or "soon to occur" ranges from zero (Barclay's New Testament, KJB, Cranmer, Geneva Bible, Tyndale, Rheims, The New Testament: English Version for the Deaf, Beck's Translation of the New Testament) to 49 times (Concordant Literal New Testament, Weymouth Version New Testament in Modern Speech). Young's literal translation of the New Testament renders 35 out of 50 along with Weymouth. So, there is a wide disparity and disagreement on how to render the word mello.[3]

---

[2] Curtis Cates, The A.D. 70 Theology, p. 38
[3] William Bell, Jr, The Re-Examination, A Review of William Jones' An Examination of the A.D. 70 Teaching, pp. 59-60.

Cates' Embarrassing Mello Backfire!

Curtis Cates attempted to disprove the imminence of mello with the *present infinitive* referring to the resurrection of the just and the unjust in Acts 24:15. He offered that the leading lexicographers of our day translate *esesthai mellein* as "…there shall be a resurrection of the dead, both of the just and the unjust". He cites the following references: *Winter and Winter, The Word Study New Testament, p. 476.* Then he argued that "This rare future infinitive, reinforced by mellein, must be translated "shall be" (cf. Acts 23:30; see *Greenlee, A Concise Exegetical Grammar of the New Testament Greek, p. 52; Pershbacker, The New Analytical Greek Lexicon, p. xxv)*. Cates makes this concluding comment. "In other words, the use of the future infinitive **does not** specify any time element between the Biblical prophetic statement and its fulfillment. Drew Leonard cited Cates as an authority claiming "the timing of those events was **extremely distant.**"[4]

However when we examine the evidence for the use of the future infinitive *esesthai,* used with the present infinitive mello, all examples of this rare form are found in the book of Acts. Only 6 occurrences are found in the NT while 14 are found in the A.T. Robertson's *A Greek Grammar of the New Testament in the Light of Historical Research,* p. 1082 Robertson lists three out of the four occurrences in Acts that are identical in structure. The fourth, Acts 23:30, cited by Cates, is not directly equivalent in structure to Acts 24:15. Robertson, states it is dependent on a participle after a past indicative. We will examine each occurrence in Acts.

Exhibit A: Acts 11:28

Then one of them, name Agabus, stood up and showed by the Spirit that there [esesthai mellein] was going to be a great famine throughout all the world, which also happened in the days of Claudius Caesar."

[4] Drew Leonard, The A.D. 70 Teaching, End of Time Southaven 2017 Lectures, Southaven Church of Christ, Southaven, MS, p. 67.

Remember, Cates said "the future infinitive does not specify any time element between the prophetic statement and its fulfillment. Well this is a prophecy. And the fulfillment is given in the very same text! How disingenuous of Cates! It's ignorance at best and dishonest at worst. Note that *"esesthai"* is the future infinitive of *"eimi"* (to be). However, *"mellein"* is the *present infinitive* of mello. It governed or limited the future time when the famine would occur. This clearly shows the imminence of famine prophesied in those days, even coming **before Jerusalem fell.** It is clearly an **imminent** demonstration and proof of mellein. **This is the equivalent construction of Acts 24:15!**

Exhibit B: Acts 27:10

Saying, 'Men, I perceive that this voyage will [esesthai mellein] end with disaster and much loss, not only of the cargo and ship, but also our lives.'"

Here again we have the *future infinitive* of **mellein** with proof in the **same context** that the loss of which Paul spoke was **imminent** and occurred during their current voyage! They shipwrecked before reaching their destination and threw the cargo overboard. Again, it is the same construction as Acts 24:15. Paul, an inspired prophet had forewarned them of imminent danger. So it was **prophecy fulfilled**. Because they listened to Paul, their lives were spared.

Exhibit C: Acts 24:15:

I have hope in God, which they themselves also accept, that there will be [esesthai mellein] a resurrection of the dead, both of the just and the unjust." (Acts 24:15)

Are we to deny the evidence above and accept Cate's shoddy scholarship on the use of this construction? Leonard bought the entire sales pitch. This is absolutely embarrassing.

Moses, Deuteronomy 32:22

Moses prophesied of Israel's last days, (Deut. 31:29; 32:29). Later he said, "For a fire is kindled in My anger, and shall burn to the lowest hell (Sheol/gehenna); It shall consume the earth with her increase, and set on fire the foundations of the mountains," (v. 22).

What is of importance is to note how specifically this prophecy relates to Judah and Jerusalem in her last days. In other words it is not a global prophecy, but a covenant concept. Moses identifies the precise generation, speaking of it as the *perverse and crooked generation,* (32:5, 20). Jesus and the apostles identified their generation as that fulfilling the description in the Song of Moses, (Matt. 12:39, 16:4 17:17 23:36, 24:34, Mk. 8:38, Acts 2:40, Phil. 2:14). Thus no other generation or people are intended.

God therefore, promised to set *Israel's* earth on fire. Judaism would be destroyed by the fire of God, meaning it would be utterly consumed. That these words do not escape a New Testament first century application is evident in the quotes made of them by the apostles. Compare:

- Fire of God's anger consumes the earth, v. 22, with Heb. 12:29; 2 Peter 3:7-10.
- The reference to "Sodom", v. 32, with Revelation 11:8.
- The judgment laid up in store v. 34, with 2 Peter 3:7.
- Vengeance is mine and recompense, v. 35a, 41, with Lk. 21:22, Rom. 12:19; Heb. 10:30.
- The day of their calamity is at hand, v. 35b, with 1 Peter 4:7, 17.
- The things to come hasten upon them, v. 35c, with 2 Peter 2:3; 3:12.
- Rejoice, O Gentiles, with His people, v. 43, with Rom. 15:10.
- He will avenge the blood of his servants, v. 43, with Rev. 18:20, 24, 19:2.
- Atonement of the land and his people, Rom. 5:11.

Here we see the source of the Apostles' reference to destruction of the earth (eretz/ge) by fire originating with Moses.

Zephaniah's Destruction by Fire and 2 Peter 3:10-12

Zephaniah prophesies of the destruction of Jerusalem by Nebuchadnezzar. He described it as the utter destruction of the earth (eretz) using the same language as Moses in Deuteronomy 32, and 2 Peter 3:10-12.

> "I will utterly consume everything from the face of the land," says the Lord; I will consume man and beast; I will consume the birds of the heavens, the fish of the sea, and the stumbling blocks along with the wicked. I will cut off man from the face of the earth says the Lord."

God said he would utterly consume the earth. Was the destruction of Jerusalem in the time of Nebuchadnezzar in the 6th century B.C., the end of all life on the planet? Does it not say He would consume man and beast and all the birds of the air and fish of the sea? Did not Moses say everything would be consumed and burned to the lowest *Sheol* by fire? Did not Peter say the earth and heavens with all the elements shall be burned, 2 Peter 3:10-12? This language is all the same and refers to the same type event both in type and antitype.

Yet, God says this prophecy refers to the Babylonian destruction of Judah and Jerusalem in 586 B.C. "I will stretch out My hand against Judah, and against all the inhabitants of Jerusalem." (Zeph. 1: 4). God did not wipe out all mankind and animals from the face of the globe in 586 B.C. This apocalyptic language figuratively describes the local judgment upon Jerusalem by the Chaldeans. "But the whole land shall be devoured by the fire of His jealousy, for He will make speedy riddance of all those who dwell in the land," (1:18). Again God says, "all the earth shall be devoured with the fire of my jealousy." (3:8).[5] Nebuchadnezzar also destroyed other nations during the time making it a "universal" or worldwide judgment, (Jer. 25:9) That language did not mean the destruction of the globe by fire.

---

[5] Other texts where "face of the earth" is used: Gen. 4:14, 41:46; 10:4-5, 15, Num. 22:5, Ezek. 34:6, Dan 8:5, Zeph. 1:2-3.

Chapter 3:
Destroyed Them All

When comparing Luke 21:34, 35 with Luke 17:26-29 and Matthew 24:37-39, it becomes clear that Luke's reference is to the flood and Sodom and Gomorrah. Though he does not explicitly mention them in this text, it becomes obvious that he alludes to them in citing the very same behavior and warning mentioned in both.

There is no question that the admonition regarding the flood of Noah follows the discussion of the destruction of Jerusalem and the end of heaven and earth in Matthew 24:35-39. In fact, the only verse separating them is verse 36, which speaks of that day and hour.

However, Luke supplies that connection in his account in chapter 17:26-28, when he implies that in both destructions the inhabitants perished in their respective last days. Does this not imply what is taught in Matthew 24:37-39? Also even where Mark omits those events altogether, the attention called to "that day and hour" which no man knew suggests the same. Thus, the flood analogy is implied in Mark and Luke's context. More than likely, Luke's account is an ellipsis.

This would therefore help us to understand the limited scope of Luke's account. It could be read as follows.

> "But take heed to yourselves, lest your hearts be weighed down with carousing, drunkenness, and cares of this life, and that Day come on you unexpectedly. "For as the days of Noah were, they were eating and drinking, marrying and giving in marriage until the day that Noah entered the ark, and the flood came and destroyed them all."

Likewise in the days of Lot: They ate, they drank, they bought, they sold, they planted, they built; but on the day that Lot went out of Sodom it rained fire and brimstone from heaven and destroyed them all." (Luke 21:34, 17:27-29)

Now, by including the verses here, they appear to fit perfectly, do no violence to the meaning of the text and make the sense of Luke's account complete. The point however is that Luke says of Sodom that God *destroyed them all* and so would it be in the days of the Son of Man. Two points are of note.

First, the phrase God "destroyed them all" does not refer to a "global" destruction of all mankind from the earth. Rather, it refers to the local or regional inhabitants of Sodom and Gomorrah. Yahweh destroyed all of those who were disobedient, i.e. those who were eating and drinking, marrying and giving in marriage before the judgment. This is true whether one accepts the usage of the text here as I've done or settles for Jesus' use of it in chapter 17.

Secondly, the last day of Lot did not mean the last tick of the clock. Time continued on from that point and yet rolls along today. So, it was neither the end of all life and chronological time, nor was it global, but local and applicable to those living in the generation of Lot.

Now, this also carries significant implications for the use of the flood, since it neither marked the end of chronological time nor all life from the planet. To use the flood as an analogy for wiping out the earth is to make an injudicious use of the event. Woods acknowledged that no such parallel exists between the destruction of the planet in Genesis 6-9 and an alleged conflagration of the material world.

> "The waters from above from above and below joined as instruments in the hands of God in the judgment upon the wicked world. It thus "perished" (apollumi), i.e., it was destroyed. It was not annihilated, for such the word does not mean. The existing order was not changed; the evils of the age were removed, and there emerged a new world cleansed from its former impurities."[6]

---

[6] Guy N. Woods, A Commentary on the Second Epistle of Peter, 1976, p. 184.

That the fall of Jerusalem is confined geographically to Judea cannot be doubted. This is not to say that others throughout the Roman Empire were not involved in or affected by its' destruction. Rome commanded legions from throughout the empire to fight against Jerusalem. Further, its universal impact is elsewhere acknowledged.

In addition, those who were in Judea were urged to flee from Judea. It makes no sense to flee from Judea if this were a global event. If the earth were burning with fire, where could anyone run to escape? However, the fact that the judgment was locally contained, does not mean its impact and influence were local. The reach of that judgment extended to Abel and the creation, Matthew 23:32-36. It affected men as far away as Athens, all of whom were commanded to repent in view of the "about to come" (mellei krinein—mello with the present infinitive] judgment upon the inhabited earth. Interestingly, the word "inhabited earth" (oikoumene) is the very same term found in Matthew 24:14, which says the gospel had to be preached to all the nations in all the inhabited earth (oikoumene) and then the end would come.

It cannot be that there were two judgments of two separate and independent inhabited earths both of which were about to come in that very same generation. The judgment about to come of Acts 17:31 is the same judgment upon Jerusalem. Paul reasoned with Felix, governor of Caesarea about righteousness, self-control and the judgment about to come, (Mellontos esesthai), Acts 24:24-26). Five things we can say about this judgment that made Felix, a non-Jew, i.e. a Gentile who lived outside of Jerusalem to shake fearfully shake in his boots.

First, this judgment could not be temporal, i.e. one that merely would terminate in A.D. 70. Felix, who lived outside of Jerusalem, would have no fear of a judgment whose scope would terminate at the fall of the temple. All he would have to do is bide his time until the temple fell, then go on about his merry way. That does not offer a reasonable explanation of a man who trembled at the thought of a coming imminent judgment.

Secondly, the judgment was not merely of a local nature. We demonstrated this above with the men of Athens (Acts 17). In addition, it's also important to note that were this judgment limited to Israel only, Paul was misguided in his mission for applying the message of repentance, salvation and judgment to this licentious Gentile. Again, it does not account for Felix's actions even in a pre-70 A.D. context. Felix easily could have reminded Paul that he was outside the boundaries of his jurisdiction and that he was not a son of Abraham. Therefore, none of the promises or predictions of wrath were in anywise related to him. However, in Romans, Paul taught in Romans, that in the Day of Judgment God would judge the secrets of men by Jesus Christ, according to the gospel. (Rom. 2:16)

Thirdly, Paul's preaching to Felix confirmed that the gospel was for all nations. Felix was a freedman, i.e. a Greek who obtained Roman citizenship through his kinsmen. The Romans were by no means members of the nation of Israel. Not only did Paul preach to Felix, but also to Agrippa and to members of Caesars's household. It is one thing to have those who voluntarily seek to join themselves to Israel. It is altogether another to evangelize them as a part of the great commission. It is the latter that Paul did under the most non-ordinary of circumstances, i.e. during his imprisonment under house arrest for two years.

Fourthly, while Greeks believed in life after death, nothing suggested that Felix was a righteousness man who believed in such tenets. In fact, from what history reports of him, was to the contrary. He was licentious, filled with lust, took bribes and was removed from office as a direct result of his misconduct. The fact that he sought for Paul often hoping Paul would pay him money for his freedom demonstrated that he had no regard for law or morality. Why then would the "judgment to come" make him tremble? We have ruled out living to the end of that judgment as a valid reason. There had to be some eternal consequence Felix would face beyond those circumstances. In other words, the gospel speaks of judgment in which he would be held accountable for his sins. Those consequences would deny him of any salvation beyond this life as well.

Finally, it demonstrated that the judgment would not be delayed. It was a judgment about to come. It had an imminent message for Felix. He had to make a decision while living if he wanted to escape it or to enjoy

God's favor. At death, the door would be permanently clothed. A judgment two thousand years away would be as if Paul mocked. Felix had to face consequences which were staring him in the face for his behavior and conduct that merited God's wrath and vengeance upon him.

Chapter 4:
All the Earth

I t is argued by Amillennialists that while Luke 21:6-32 speaks of Jerusalem's destruction in A.D. 70, verses 34-35 speak of a yet future
judgment and destruction to come upon all the earth. This effort
seeks to evade the force of Jesus' words which state that all things written
were fulfilled with Jerusalem's fall in A.D. 70. He taught that all came
to pass before that first century generation passed, (Luke 21:20-22, 32).

Ted J. Clarke, in his presentation at the "Ready to Answer" 18th
Annual Mid-West Lectureship, 2000, advanced the following argument:

> Luke 21:34-36 shows that this latter section was not speaking of an event
> connected with the local destruction of Jerusalem. There Jesus said, "For as a
> snare shall it come upon all who dwell on the face of the whole earth" (verse
> 35). Matthew 24:34 says that all the signs and events of which Jesus had previously
> spoken in verses 4-33 would happen to "this generation," the Jews to whom
> He then was speaking. It is a fact of history that Jerusalem was destroyed in
> A.D. 70. However, the destruction of Jerusalem was not the "end of the
> world." "Heaven and earth" did not pass away. Jesus said regarding that "day
> and hour" no one knew except God. Then He went on to speak of what it
> would be like when He did come in judgment "on all who dwell on the face
> of the whole earth" (Luke 21:35; Matthew 24:37-25:46). This division of
> Matthew 24 into verses 4-34 dealing with the destruction of Jerusalem, and
> verses 35-51 referring to the judgment connected with Christ's second coming
> absolutely destroys the A.D. 70 doctrine. Upon close examination, the
> argument fails to deliver the desired conclusion of a yet future return of Christ
> following the A.D. 70 event."[7]

[7] Ted J. Clark http://www.kccofc.org/39th/Lectures/2000%20Manuscripts/-Clarke%20-
%20AD%2070.PDF

Does the Lord mean an event future to the destruction of Jerusalem in A.D. 70 when speaking of the **whole earth?** Clarke cites three reasons why he believes these verses apply to our future and not to a past event.

First, he says that no one knows the "day and hour," of the event except the Father. Secondly, he says it is a judgment that would come upon all who dwell on the face of the whole earth. Thirdly, he claims that it represents a division of the A.D. 70 coming of Christ from a future coming (as that proposed in the dividing of Matthew 24). He concludes that this absolutely destroys the A.D. 70 doctrine. We intend to show how each of these assertions is false and fails to support the desired conclusion, i.e. that Christ's return is yet future.

Chapter 5:
That Day and Hour

No man knows the day and the hour. Luke does not mention the phrase, *"but of that day and hour no man knows"* as does Matthew and Mark. That does not mean that the idea is not present in the text. Clarke correctly deduces the idea from the language of surprise suggested by the unexpectedness indicated in the text. Normal life continued without interruption allowing for its surprise.

The idea of not knowing the day is prophetic and relates directly to the destruction of Jerusalem in A.D. 70. This is confirmed by two passages from the Old Covenant. The first is the Son of Moses, (Deuteronomy 32) where Moses speaks of Judah's last days, when God takes vengeance on the perverse and crooked generation, (Deut. 32:5, 20).

In fact, Jesus draws from that very context to pronounce his judgment upon the Jews. Four times in Deuteronomy 32, he mentions that God would take vengeance on the terminal generation of Israel, (Deut. 32:35, 41, 43). Compare Luke 21:20-22. Twice in Moses' prophecy, God says that Judah would not know the time of the event.

> "For they are a nation void of counsel, nor is there any understanding in them. Oh, that they were wise and understood this, that they would consider their latter end!" (v. 28-29)

Jesus quotes directly from this verse and laments because Judah did not know the time of her visitation i.e. judgment.

> "Now as He drew near, he saw the city and wept over it, saying, 'If you had known, even you, especially in this your day, the things that make for your peace! But now they are hidden from your eyes," (Luke 19:41-44)

Not only did Judah not know the day and hour, they did not know the "generation" because of their unbelief. The reason Judah did not know the "day and hour" of her visitation is because God said the event was "laid up in store with Me, sealed up among My treasures?" (Deut. 32:34) In other words, God had not revealed the "day and hour" of the event. It was His secret, stored up like precious treasure in His own mind and daily guarded as if by a military command guarding a top secret.

Zechariah 14:7

The prophet writes concerning the day of the Lord. His context is the destruction of Jerusalem in A.D. 70. God would gather all nations to battle against Jerusalem, v. 2. It would be one day which is known to the LORD—neither day nor night, but at evening time it shall happen that it will be light." (v. 7) It is at that time that "living waters" would flow from Jerusalem, v. 8, at which time the LORD would be King over all the earth. This cannot be a mere reference to the land of Israel, unless all kings lived in the land of Palestine. "All the earth" here refers to Christ's sovereignty over all the nations, when he became "King of kings and Lord of lords." (Rev. 11:15-18) That is clearly the time of judgment upon the nations, for the time of God's wrath had come for the nations to be judged, the resurrection of the dead, the time God would give reward to his servants the prophets and the destruction of those who destroyed the land.

Additional reasons Zechariah cannot possibly be speaking of a day that ends all life on the planet are found in the aftermath of the destruction. In verses 16-20, he says that all the nations which came up against Jerusalem, **shall go up to worship the King**, the Lord of hosts and **keep the Feast of Tabernacles**. He specifically names Egypt and then categorically includes **all the nations.**

These events could not possibly be given a scenario where the earth is burned and destroyed. Yet, in verse 7, he says that when the Lord comes with all his saints, the following occurs: "It shall come to pass in that day that there will be no light; the lights will diminish. It shall be one day which is known to the Lord—neither day nor night. But at evening time it shall happen that it will be light." (Zech. 14:6-7).

Jesus quotes from Zechariah 12:7 in Matthew 24:36. See also Mark 13:32. He clearly discusses the destruction of Jerusalem within the first century generation, Matthew 24:34 drawing upon Moses' words from Deuteronomy 32:28-29.

> "For they are a nation void of counsel, nor is there any understanding in them. Oh, that they were wise, that they understood this, that they would consider their latter end!"

Jesus cited the text in Luke 19:42 further accenting Israel's ignorance of her time of visitation.

> "Now as He drew near, He saw the city and wept over it, saying, "If you had known, even you, especially in this your day, the things that make for your peace! But now they are hidden from your eyes. For days will come upon you when your enemies will build and embankment around you, surround you and close you in on every side, and level you, and your children within you, to the ground; and they will not leave in you one stone upon another, because you did not know the time of your visitation. "

Moses spoke of the destruction of Judah and Jerusalem in her last days as a time that only the Lord knew. Yet God said that event concerned Israel in their last days, Deut. 31:28-32:43. Therefore, the day that only God knew referred to a time when he would bring destruction upon the Jewish nation in A.D. 70.

Things Equal to the Same Thing Are Equal To Each Other

We have established that Deuteronomy 32:28-29 and v. 34, referred to a day only known by God in the last days, i.e. sealed up in his treasures. But the day of the Lord in Zechariah 14:7, which also was in the last days, was a day known to the Lord, hence sealed up in his treasures. Therefore, the day of the Lord in Zechariah 14:7, equals the time of the judgment in Deuteronomy 32:34.

Now since the unknown day of the Lord in Zechariah 14:7 equals the unknown day of the Lord in Matthew 24:36, and Mark 13:32, and since they equal the *second* coming of Christ, then Deuteronomy 32:28-

29 and 35, equal the second coming of Christ. But the events of Deuteronomy 32 speak of the last days of Judah and their end in 70A.D. That is proof positive that the destruction of Jerusalem equates in time with Jesus' second coming. Things equal to the same thing are equal to each other.

Identifying the Source of Sophistry

The fallacy of the "that day and hour argument" is the failure of distinguishing between the "generation" identified in the prophecy of Deuteronomy 32 per verses 5 and 20, and the precise day and hour. In both prophecies, the *precise generation* **is identified** while the *precise day and hour* **is not**. So, the futurists usually reason that because everything is not known about the time of an event, nothing is known; or because the precise time is unknown, the general time cannot be known.

Consider this illustration. If a boy's father tells him that he's going to take him fishing next year what can the boy tell his friends about the time of the fishing trip? Can he tell them the day and hour? Will it be on a Friday at noon, a Saturday morning or on a Sunday evening? He has no clue. All the father only told him was that they were going fishing next year. That's all the boy could reveal at the time because that is all he was told.

The language of Christ is similar. At the time of his incarnation he revealed *the generation*, but His Father had not at the time revealed *the day and hour*. Yet, that does not mean, that the event would not occur in that generation. Later, God revealed to Christ the time of judgment, saying that it was near. "The Revelation of Jesus Christ, which God gave Him to show His servants—things which must shortly take place". And He sent and signified it by His angel to His servant John. Therefore, what Christ did not know during His ministry was revealed to Him by the Father after His ascension to the throne.

The Feast of Trumpets

There is another contextual dynamic of which most are not aware that underlies the text in Matthew 24:36. It is the *Feast of Trumpets*. This is one of the eight Jewish Festivals about which there were some unique details, readily recognized by an ancient Jewish audience but which are almost totally lost on a contemporary audience today who does not value the Old Testament as a key to interpreting the new.

The Feast of Trumpets was the only one of the seven Jewish festivals which occurred on the first day of the month. The first fall feast was *Feast of Trumpets,* also known as *Rosh Hashanah.* There were *three* fall festivals. The spring festivals of *Passover, Unleavened Bread and Pentecost* were dress rehearsals for Jesus' first coming. *The Feast of Trumpets, The Day of Atonement (Yom Kippur) and the Feast of Tabernacles* were dress rehearsals for Jesus' second coming.

These were also called holy convocations. Mark Biltz says, "Remember, a convocation is not only an assembly at an appointed time but also a dress rehearsal.[8] The spring feasts were the *grain* feasts, for harvesting of cereals such as barley and wheat. The fall festivals were the *fruit and vine* feasts. In Hosea's prophecy of the last days, he spoke of the fall festivals in the following:

> "It shall come to pass in that day that I will answer," says the LORD; I will answer the heavens, and they shall answer the earth. The earth shall answer with grain, with new wine, and with oil; they shall answer Jezreel." (Hos. 32:21-22)

The new wine and oil is the harvest of grape vines and olive trees, etc. In the book of Revelation chapter 14, we see a harvest of grapes. This refers to the feast of Trumpets. It is the feast of judgment. The feast of trumpets came every year, and therefore the Israel knew the meaning of this feast.

One unique fact about the feast of Trumpets is that it is the only feast day which came on the first day of the month. In other words, it came at the arrival of the *new moon.* This presented a problem. Before

---

[8] Mark Biltz, Blood Moons: Decoding the Imminent Heavenly Signs, Kindle Version

the trumpet or shofar could be sounded or blown, two witnesses had to confirm the first sighting of the new moon. This was the **"day that was not known"** in Israel. The priests could not sound the shofar until they received confirmation that the new moon had been sighted.

Note also according to Biltz, there were several names for the Feast of Trumpets. It was called:

- The time of Jacob's Trouble (The Day of the Lord)
- Yom HaDin (Day of Judgment/The Opening of the Books/Opening of the Gates)
- Yom HaKeseh (The Hidden Day)
- Ha Kiddushin/Nesuin (Wedding of the Messiah)
- HaMelech (Coronation of the Messiah)[9]

Anyone familiar with the end times events would recognize the significance of these names and their relationship to eschatological themes. The Biblical name for Rosh Hashanah is *Yom Teruah*, translated as *"Day of Blowing."* The word blowing is translated from "teruah."

> And in the seventh month, on the first day of the month, you shall have a holy convocation. You shall do no customary work. For you it is a day of blowing the trumpets. (Num. 29:1)

This same association can be seen in 1 Thessalonians 4:16.

> "For the Lord Himself will descend from heaven with a shout, with the voice of an archangel, and with the trumpet of God, and dead in Christ will rise first."

Biltz remarks, "This is telling us the resurrection of the dead will happen at the Feast of Trumpets!" He is correct.

We see this very connection in Matthew 24:31.

> "And He will send His angels with a great sound of a trumpet, and they will gather together His elect from the four winds, from one end of heaven to the other".

The sound of the trumpet and the gathering together of the elect from the four winds is the resurrection. Further, proof is seen by comparing Matthew 24:31, with Matthew 8:11-12, and Luke 13:24-28.

---

[9] Ibid

This means that Jesus placed the "day that was hidden" not only in verse 36, but for those who know the meaning of the Feast of Trumpets, the Lord also positioned it **in verse 31!** That is the verse which precedes verse 34 that is almost universally agreed to be the Parousia or coming of the Lord upon Jerusalem in A.D. 70! That means that the argument for dividing Matthew 24 at verse 36 can no longer be advanced with innocence. Since the Feast of Trumpets is the time of the resurrection, and since the time of the resurrection equals the judgment, the coming of the Lord and the arrival of the eternal kingdom, (2 Tim. 4:1), then all occurred within the generation presently living in the time of Christ, for it could not pass away until all were fulfilled.

Chapter 6:
Unknown and Unexpected Judgment

The above past judgments of Noah and Lot, both of which were likened to Jesus' coming, were unexpected by the wicked or unbelievers. However, because the "day and hour" was not known did not mean the event would not occur or that it would prevent its occurrence. Lack of knowledge does not equal lack of occurrence.

Luke says in the days of Noah, the people ate, drank, married and gave in marriage and **knew not** until the flood came, (Luke 17:26-27; Matt. 24:37-39). Their ignorance did not prevent the flood from occurring. However, they were forewarned as Noah told them a flood would come in their lifetime. Noah knew the generation. He knew the event would happen in his lifetime. He did not know the day and hour. (Gen 6:14-18; 7:1)

Seven days before the flood, God revealed to Noah that it would occur within 7 days, (Gen. 7:4). However, he did not reveal this to the wicked and they were destroyed. The same happened in the time of Lot. The people ate, drank, sold and planted, but knew nothing until the Lord rained fire and brimstone from heaven, (Luke 17:28-29).

Did the fact of the people's ignorance mean that the event did not occur? Did the fact of the ignorance of the unbelieving Jew's mean that Christ did not come in A.D. 70? Did the fact that they did not know the time of their visitation, i.e. the day and hour, mean the event did not occur? To this day many are ignorant of Christ's coming in A.D. 70, yet it does not mean it did not occur.

We have shown that not knowing "the day and hour" was prophesied in the Old Covenant. We examined the Jewish festival of the Feast of Trumpets as the background of Jesus' teaching of Matt. 24:36 in 24:31. Thus to claim the day has not occurred is to teach that the Law and the Prophets are yet unfulfilled and that Judaism and its feast days are yet operable. How does that work in a Christian paradigm? Lastly, we also showed one's ignorance of the event did not mean it did not occur.

Apocalyptic Hermeneutic

The hermeneutic or method of interpretation for the apostles demonstrates that they taught nothing about the end time, i.e. resurrection, the coming of the Lord and judgment that was not taught in the Law and the Prophets. In other words, their end time or last days doctrine is the message of the prophets. "But this I confess to you, that according to the Way which they call a sect, so I worship the God of my fathers, believing all things which are written in the Law and in the Prophets. I have hope in God which they themselves also accept, that there will be a resurrection of the dead, both of the just and the unjust." (Acts 24:14-15) Here again Paul uses mello with the present infinitive, i.e. mellein esesthai, is about to be.

Therefore, Paul taught nothing about the end time that was not found in the Law and the Prophets. Jesus said the same when He stated not one jot or tittle would in anywise pass from the Law till all were fulfilled. That included the passing of heaven and earth. Thus, to argue that the Law passed away at the cross would mean that Israel's last days of judgment and vengeance happened in A.D. 30, versus A.D. 70. Yet, we have demonstrated that the prophets of Deuteronomy 32 apply to Israel's destruction in A.D. 70. Therefore, the law or Old Covenant could not end before that time.

Chapter 7:
The Whole Earth Argument

Clarke reasoned that Luke 21:35 cannot be speaking of Jerusalem's destruction in A.D. 70 because it speaks of events which would come upon those dwelling on the face of the whole earth. We suggest this too is a fallacy. The Greek rendering of this phrase is (pasas tes ges) and means "all the land". Now that we have shown that Luke does not divide the chapter by virtue of the "unknown day" of the Lord; that alone destroys Clarke's reasoning. Nevertheless, the chapter does not divide by the use of "all the land".

In verses 23 and 26, Jesus says that distress would come upon the land (tes ges) and befall the inhabited earth, (te oikoumene). These are the same terms used when Paul said that the gospel had been preached in "all the world". However, the apostle uses the same identical wording of Luke 21:35 to speak of the spread of the gospel by the apostles in the first century, in direct fulfillment of Matt. 24:14 which clearly refers to A.D. 70.

This is devastating and absolutely destroys the contention that pasas tes ges (all the world) refers to a yet future cataclysm. Note: "But I say, have they not heard? Yes indeed: "Their sound has gone out to all the earth, (pasan ten gen) and their words to the ends of the world" [perata tes oikoumenes], (Rom. 10:18)

If the use of pasas tes (all the earth) means a future time in Luke 21:35, then it would mean a future time in Romans 10:18! Will futurists deny the words of the Holy Spirit and charge Paul as a false teacher when he said the gospel had gone to all the earth? Is that an event *yet to happen* in our day? Is it future? If so, then the destruction of Jerusalem has not yet occurred!

Next, Paul cites Deuteronomy 32:21, to show that the language applies to his day, when the Gentiles come in to Israel's blessings provoking them to jealousy in Judah's last days. "But I say, did Israel not know? First Moses says: 'I will provoke you to jealousy by those who are not a nation, I will move you to anger by a foolish nation,'" (Rom. 10:19). Compare Rom. 11:11, 14.

What is interesting is that in the Apocalypse, John writes of the end time events saying that the "hour of trial" was about to come on the whole world (holes oikoumene) i.e. whole inhabited earth, to test those who dwell upon the land. (Rev. 3:10) Now if it comes upon the **whole** inhabited earth to test those who dwell on the earth, would it not be going to all the earth? Would the events test those who do not dwell on the earth or inhabited places?

Now, here's the rub. If the inhabited earth of Luke 21:26, does not include the same **whole** inhabited earth of Matthew 24:14; Romans 10:18 and Revelation 3:10, then it means the Revelation message affects the whole inhabited earth while Luke refers only to 70 A.D. But, if that logic is sound, then it would discredit the "all the land" argument of Luke 21:35.

Clarke argues that Luke's all the earth (land) means a future universal coming to destroy the world. Since the trying of those who dwell on the earth does not use the word "pasas" or "all" the land, it must refer to something less than all. However, if it's less than all, then the Revelation message cannot be referent to a yet future end time coming of Christ. In other words consider the following syllogism:

Omission of "all" [pasas] from the phrase "all the earth" means less than the whole earth per the futurist argument. An event which is less than the whole earth is not a universal or future end times event. Therefore, Revelation 3:10 does not describe a future universal event.

On the other hand, if the Revelation message would try all those who dwelled on the earth void of the use of all [pasas] then this negates the argument in Luke 21:35, that "all the earth" (land) can only mean the whole earth in our future. Matthew 24:14 and Romans 10:18 clearly are first century events.

We suggest that the term *all the inhabited earth* is identical to the phrase *"on the earth"* in Revelation 3:10 and means the same. Both refer to the A.D. 70 fall of Jerusalem as seen when comparing Matthew, Luke and Revelation.

Matthew 24:14

In this text Jesus commanded the apostles to preach to the nations, saying, "And this gospel of the kingdom will be preached in "all the world" as a witness to all the nations, and then the end will come."

The phrase used here for "all the world" is *hole tes oikoumene*, (gk.) i.e. the whole inhabited earth. However, when Paul speaks of the fulfillment of this text, he says the gospel had been preached to all the earth. This equates with the phrases Revelation 3:10. Now there is no question that Jesus uses the term whole inhabited earth in Mathew 24:14.

Equally clear is that he speaks of events leading up to and pertaining to the A.D. 70 destruction of Jerusalem in the last days of the Jewish era. If this phrase used for the whole inhabited earth refers to the fall of Jerusalem, then what about its use in Revelation 3:10?

All the inhabited earth per Rev. 3:10 equals the all the inhabited earth of Matthew 24:14. But the whole inhabited earth of Matthew 24:14 refers to the A.D. 70 destruction of Jerusalem. Therefore, the whole inhabited earth of Revelation 3:10 likewise applies to the destruction of Jerusalem in 70 A.D.

In further proof of this conclusion note that Matthew 24:14 is likewise parallel to Luke 21:23 and verse 26. **Matthew 24:14, "in all the inhabited earth" refers to the destruction of Jerusalem in A.D. 70. But the whole inhabited earth" of Matthew 24:14 is parallel to the "inhabited earth" of Luke 21:26. Therefore, the whole inhabited earth of Matthew 24:14 and the inhabited earth of Luke 21:26 are identical and refer to A.D. 70.**

Thus we have proved that both Revelation 3:10 and Matthew 24:14 which speak of the whole inhabited earth are parallel passages to Luke 21:26 which omits pasas (all). We have proved that "all the habited earth" of Revelation 3:10 likewise is parallel to the "the whole earth" in Luke 21:35.

Things equal to the same thing are equal to one another. Since Matthew 24:14, refers to the A.D. 70 destruction of Jerusalem, and since it is parallel to both Revelation 3:10 and Luke 21:26 and verse 35, then all passages refer to the destruction of Jerusalem in A.D. 70.

How then can it be denied that "distress upon the earth" (land) in Luke 21:23, means something different than in verse 34? Or that the "inhabited earth" of Luke 21:26, means less than "the whole inhabited earth of Revelation 3:10? If it means the same, then both Revelation 3:10 and Luke 21:26 are parallel. Since Clarke agrees that Luke 21:6-32, refers to Jerusalem's fall in A.D. 70, then his entire position crumbles.

Revelation 14:6

"Then I saw another angel flying in the midst of heaven, having the everlasting gospel to preach to those who dwell on the earth—to every nation, tribe, tongue, and people.

This passage omits the words "all the earth (land). Yet it is an everlasting message to be preached to every nation, tribe, tongue and people. If it is true that to omit the word all from a text means it is not a yet future universal event, then here is proof positive that John does not speak about an event beyond the first century. But the message here is the same as that of Matthew 24:14, i.e. to preach to all the nations. Therefore, it refers to the events of 70 A.D. What one does to one of these texts must be done to all. Either they all are a universal future event, or none are. If all are then one must say that Jesus never spoke a single word about a coming in 70A.D.

On the other hand, if all refer to A.D. 70 and we have proven they do, then it must be admitted that Jesus spoke never a word about a yet future coming to destroy the entire planet. However, we have shown that both the inclusion of and the omission of "whole" (pasas from all the world, all the land, and all the inhabited earth, mean the same.

Chapter 8:
The Kingdom of God

L uke records the coming of the kingdom to be at hand in connection with Jerusalem's fall in A.D. 70. This is yet future to Pentecost, but definitely falls within that generation. Revelation likewise speaks of events that were at hand and shortly to come to pass, Rev. 1:1 and 3. One such event was the coming of the kingdom in judgment, 11:15-18 again showing the message of the two books are one and the same. We have shown this time was A.D. 70 therefore, the coming of the kingdom reached consummation in A.D. 70.

In addition, as in Luke 21:20-22, and verse 32, Jesus mentions a time statement limited all events of the chapter to A.D. 70, the Revelation message also limits the time to A.D. 70 in its message of imminence.

Same Audience

Finally, Jesus' directs the entire message in Luke to the same first century audience. There is no indication that he changes and speaks of a future generation. However, when comparing Moses' words in Deuteronomy 32:7 God makes clear that He addresses a future generation. He says after many generations from Moses, the events would happen. Not once does Jesus or the apostles use such terms when speaking of the end. Further, when God means a different time or generation than that to which he speaks he knows how to express that as well.

Abraham

When God spoke of Israel inheriting the land and of the Abrahamic promise, he specifically advised the patriarch those events would not occur in his day. Following the details of the prophecy about the land, God says this to Abraham.

> "Now as for you, you shall go to your fathers in peace; you shall be buried at a good old age. But in the fourth generation they shall return here, for the iniquity of the Amorites is not yet complete." (Gen. 15:15-16)

In addition, when the prophets inquired about whether the end times events would occur in their day, they asked God when those events would occur.

Daniel

Again, God speaks to Daniel who inquires of the time for the fulfillment of the end times wonders.

> "Although I heard, I did not understand. Then I said, 'My lord, what shall be the end of these things?" And he said, 'Go your way, Daniel, for the words are closed up and sealed till the time of the end." (Dan. 12:8-9) See also verse 13.

Peter

When God spoke to the apostles of the things which the prophets saw, he told them as he said above, they were not for the patriarchs or the O.T. prophets, but they were for the apostles and the N.T. first century church!

> "Of this salvation the prophets have inquired and searched carefully, who prophesied of the grace that would come **to you**, searching what, or what manner of time, the Spirit of Christ who was in them was indicating when He testified beforehand the sufferings of Christ and the glories that would follow. To them it was revealed that, **not to themselves**, <u>but to us</u> they were ministering the things which now have been reported **to you** through those who have preached the gospel to you by the Holy Spirit sent from heaven— things which angels desire to look into. Therefore, gird up the loins of **your** mind, be sober, and rest **your** hope fully upon the grace that is to be brought **to you** at the revelation of Jesus Christ." (1 Peter. 1:11-13). Emp. Mine WHB.

The same is true for those in Luke 21:35. Jesus addressed his immediate contemporary audience and saying the events were coming upon them. "But [you] take heed to yourselves, lest your hearts be weighted down with carousing, drunkenness, and cares of this life, and that Day come on you unexpectedly.

Nor is there any reason therefore to take the word "those" of verse 35, to refer to another remote generation far removed from that of the apostles. Rather it refers to their contemporary counterparts who lived in the same generation but who refused to accept Christ and the apostles' words to turn from their unrighteousness in true repentance.

Chapter 9:
Which Heaven and Earth?

I n this segment, we now consider what is meant by the passing of heaven and earth. We suggest the terms are covenantal versus cosmic. In the context of both the entire book of Hebrews and the particular text of 1:10-12, the contrast is that between the Old and the New Covenants.

I would take the reference in chapter 1:10-12, to refer, not to the beginning in Genesis 1, but to the "beginning" of the Old Covenant creation, as contrasted with the new creation in Christ, designated by the reference to that which is unchangeable, permanent and enduring.

In other words, "You, Lord, in the beginning laid the foundation of the earth and the heavens are the work of your hands." (We acknowledge this quote from Psalms 102:25-27). However, note that this heaven and earth is that which perishes and waxes old like a garment versus the "Lord" who remains. Hence, "Lord who remains" is by metonymy[10] "another" name for the "new heaven and earth".

The pronoun "they" refers back to the heaven and earth which perishes and whose foundation was laid in the beginning. I would therefore conclude that the "beginning" here is the beginning of the Old Covenant of Moses. That beginning according to Galatians 4:21 and Hebrews 12:18, Ex. 19, is **Sinai**, not Genesis one.

I see this same contrast in Isaiah 51:6:

"Lift up your eyes to the heavens, and look on the earth beneath. For the heavens will vanish away like smoke, the earth will grow old like a garment,

---

[10] D. R Dungan, Hermeneutics, p. 270. Metonymy is from the Greek words meta, change, and onoma, name, hence a change of name; the employment of one name or word for another.

and those who dwell in it will die in like manner; But my salvation will be forever, and my righteousness shall not be abolished."

Again, we have a contrast between Christ, in whom is our salvation that remains forever and who is not destroyed, versus a creation (heaven and earth) that would be destroyed. Now this would mean that we have from the above, at least two "beginnings of creation" one for the Old Covenant and one for the New Covenant. God is definitely called the "Creator" of Jacob/Israel, Isa. 43:1, 15, as He would create a new heaven and earth, i.e. new Israel, thus new beginning. See Isa. 65:17-18.

Foundations

It is argued that because Hebrews 1:10 refers to the "foundations" of the earth that it is a clear designation for the physical universe. However, we suggest, based on Scriptures that will follow, that every time the concept of destruction the world is mentioned in Scripture, it is always *non-literal* and instead is an apocalyptic or figurative reference.

How has God used the term "foundations in the past? Has it always referred to that only which was material in nation? In 2 Samuel 22, David spoke a Psalm after his deliverance from Saul. I would suggest reading the entire chapter but here is the section toward which we focus some attention.

"In my distress I called upon the Lord, and cried out to my God' He heard my voice from His temple, and my cry entered His ears. Then the earth shook and trembled; the foundations of heaven quaked and were shaken, because he was angry. Smoke went up from His nostrils, and devouring fire from His mouth; coals were kindled by it. He bowed the heavens also, and came down with darkness under His feet. (vv. 7-10).

The point here is that such language is figurative.

I am aware that Psalm 18 uses "hills" instead of heavens and some translations use "hills" or mountains. However, they spoke of **"bending the heavens"** which in essence is the same idea. Further, in a context that cannot be dismissed as referring to Israel in Sinai, the prophet Isaiah wrote:

"Oh, that You would rend the heavens! That you would come down! That the mountains might shake at Your Presence—As fire burns brushwood, and fire causes water to boil to make your name known to your adversaries, that the nations may tremble at Your presence! When You did awesome things for which we did not look, You came down, the mountains shook at Your presence, for "since" the beginning of the world [some translations and scholars render, from time of old] men have not heard nor hearkened to, and eye has not seen a God who did such marvelous things." (Isa. 64:1-4)

Why would God say, men had never seen what he did "in the beginning" of the material or natural creation when there were no men present to see it? That is a truism. It is apparent that God is speaking of a time "in history". Hence, he says "since" or "from" the beginning, meaning a point away from the beginning" not before it when they did not exist. No man of all the gods they saw had seen a God who comes down from the heavens, shakes the mountains, and makes a covenant with his people. Paul uses the language in the same manner to speak of the new covenant foundations God was laying in which he would shake the earth again in consummation of the New Covenant (1 Cor. 2:9-13, 1 Cor. 3:10-11) which is precisely what is occurring per Hebrews 1:10-12, 12:18-28.

Job assures us that man did not exist before the beginning of the creation.

"Now prepare yourself like a man; I will question you, and you shall answer Me. Where were you when I laid the foundations of the earth? Tell Me, if you have understanding. Who determined its measurements? Surely you know! Or who stretched the line upon it? To what were its foundations fastened? Or who laid its cornerstone, when the morning stars sang together, and all the sons of God shouted for joy? "(Job. 38:3-7; Jn. 1:1)

God specifically questioned Job about his "pre-creation knowledge. Job could not answer. No man could answer because no man was there. Why, then would God speak of anything entering into the mind of man before man was created. It makes absolutely no sense to refer the "foundations" in Heb. 1:10-12 to the material creation on that point alone. However, that is not the only point, nor is it the strongest reason to reject it as an argument.

David writes in the 90th Psalm,

"LORD you have been our dwelling place in all generations. Before the mountains were brought forth or ever you had formed the earth and the world, even from everlasting to everlasting, You are God. (Psa. 90:2)

If God was God before the mountains were brought forth, and since the mountains were created before man, then God was also God before man was created. To say it another way, God was God before the mountains were brought forth. The mountains were brought forth before man was created. Therefore, God was God before man was created. Thus, there was no man present to see that God laid the foundations of the material creation.

However, as we shall see, men were present before God laid the foundations of the Old Covenant heavens and earth. In like manner, men were present before God laid the foundations of the new heavens and earth. Just as there was a beginning within time for the new heavens and earth, there was a beginning within time for the Old Covenant heavens and earth.

God Made the Ages

Compare John 1:1 with Hebrews 1:10-12. In Hebrews 1:10, the phrase "in the beginning" is **not** the same as that found in John 1:1, "en arche" but a different phrase, "kat' (from kata) archas". Is there contextual evidence that this phrase might be used differently than "in the beginning". We believe so and in the very same chapter.

Note Hebrews 1:2, the word is "ages" not "physical world". On the meaning of "kata" Robertson's Greek Grammar of the New Testament says "scholarship consensus is that the word generally means "down" and in such phrases as above is accompanied by "apo", from or away from, since (pp. 605-609)[11]. Thus, from Robertson's comments, we see that when "kata" is used, and especially when accompanied by apo (from or since), it means a point or time away from, after or down from the beginning, and not before that time.

---

[11] John A.T. Robertson, Word Pictures of the New Testament, Broadman Press, pp. 605-609.

End of the Ages

In Hebrews 9:26 the writer spoke of **"in the end of the ages"** to refer to the last days of the Old Covenant world in which Jesus died. Jesus was "born" of a woman, born under the law". "He then would have had to suffer often since the foundation of the world; but now once at the end of the ages, He has appeared to put away sin by the sacrifice of Himself. (Heb. 9:26) It is very important to understand what we have in this verse. First, it is clearly in a context that has mentioned the "worldly sanctuary" (cosmikon), (9:1). I point this out to show the connection of the term cosmos with the Jewish temple. The entire chapter is about the temple and sacrificial systems of Moses and Christ.

This by the way is also the emphasis of Hebrews chapter one, noted by the priestly work of Christ in "purging our sins". That calls attention to his priesthood. Thus, from the very first verses in Hebrews chapter one, a contrast between the Old Tabernacle system and New Temple is established.

Old and New Tabernacles

Christ's throne is a priestly throne, i.e. a house not made with men's hands (Dan. 2:34, 44-45; 8:14 Zech. 6:12-13). Thus, any mention of the throne or kingdom in Hebrews and elsewhere in the Scriptures must keep the "house not made with hands" i.e. the heavenly tabernacle in view.

Again, Daniel is the first to mention the *house not made with hands* and he specifically associates that terminology with the *kingdom of God*. It is a point of which **too little emphasis** is given, even in the study of Covenant Eschatology.

> "You watched while a stone was cut out without hands, which struck the image on its feet of iron and clay, and broke them in pieces." (Dan. 2:34) Note the interpretation of this statement in verse 45. "Inasmuch as you saw that the stone was cut out of the mountain without hands, and that it broke in pieces the iron, the bronze, the clay, the silver, and the gold—the great God has made known to the king what will come to pass after this. The dream is certain and its interpretation is sure."

Daniel's reference is to the kingdom that he cited in verse 44. All the arguments following chapter one have the two priesthoods i.e. that of Christ and Moses as their underlying premise and contrast.

Hebrews 9:26 and Kata

In Hebrews the ninth chapter, verse 26, a similar construction is used of the same phrase that we find in 1:10. It is not the same as the one above mentioned at the beginning of John's gospel, namely, "in the beginning" [en arche]. Rather, it is "kat' [kata] archas" and appears with the term "apo" [apo kataboles kosmou], from the foundation of the cosmos. According to Robertson's Word studies and comments on Hebrews 4:3, this identical phrase is found. Robertson comments, "Katabole, a late word from kataballo usually laying the foundation of a house in the literal sense". Vol. V, p 361).[12]

Foundation of the Jewish World

Now when we look at how the phrase is contrasted with the "end of the ages" it is quite clear that in Hebrews it is use to speak of the foundation of the Jewish world. The context is the offering of sacrifices by the High Priests of the Old Covenant system. Unless the Levitical priests were offering sacrifices "in the beginning" of the creation" it would make no sense in the context to contrast it with the "consummation of the ages" i.e. sunteleia ton aionon". See also Heb. 9:11, where a contrast with the Levitical sacrifices is made with the *new creation.*

> "It [the first tabernacle, v. 8] was symbolic for the present time in which both gifts and sacrifices are offered which cannot make him who performed the service perfect in regard to the conscience—concerned only with foods and drinks, various washings, and fleshly ordinances imposed until the time of reformation. But Christ came as High Priest of the good things [about] to come, with the greater and more perfect tabernacle not made with hands, that is, not of this creation." (Heb. 9:9-11).

---

[12] Ibid, p. 361

Thus we see the two creations contrasted. The Levitical creation expressed in the first temple made with hands, and the second creation under Christ as High Priest according to the order of Melchizedek, "made without hands" hence not of this (Levitical) creation or system.

It therefore makes perfect logical sense to speak of the "beginning or foundation of the Jewish world/age and the consummation of the ages.[13] But why are ages plural? For a long time this bothered me. The first solution I found that made sense was from Bullinger. He said that the ages are used in the plural as a figure of speech, called "heterosis of number". This is where the plural is used for the singular and visa versa, noted by E. W. Bullinger in his massive work, *Figures of Speech Used in the Bible.*

This use of the plural for ages is only found in the writings of Paul. From 1 Corinthians 10:11, Paul writes that the end of the ages (plural) had come upon his generation. Whether the term is plural or singular, the terminal point for these ages is the first century generation. It makes no sense at all to speak of the consummation of the Christian age, i.e. the age to come which had not yet arrived. Certainly the end of the Christian age had not come upon Paul's generation. Interestingly, in Ephesians, we have the plural also used for the age to come. After speaking of the age to come in Ephesians 1:21, a few verses later, Paul speaks of the ages to come. Compare the two verses.

> Far above all principality and might and dominion, and every name that is named, not only in this age but also in that which is to come. (Eph. 1;21)

> That in the ages to come, He might show the exceeding riches of His grace in His kindness toward us in Christ Jesus. (Eph. 2:7)

Either the phrase "age to come" and "ages to come" are used as a "heterosis of number" or the age to come is made up sub-ages all of which ended in the first century generation and a new set of sub-ages began within the new age to come. Either way, the outcome is the same. They are all concurrently running together whether under the Old Covenant or the New Covenant. Another possible reason is that the plural is used for emphasis which is very probable.

---

[13] Ethelbert W. Bullinger, Figures of Speech Uses in the Bible, "Heterosis of Number", p. 555.

Finally, note that Hebrews contrasts cosmos in the first part of the text, with ages in the second. This is common in his writings where he interchanges the two. See 1 Corinthians 1:20 and 3:18.

Psalm 102:25 and the Septuagint

The Septuagint (LXX) renders Psalm 102:25 in precisely the same manner, "kat' arche gen' (in the beginning of the earth or "land", meaning the land of Israel. David had already spoken of God's promise of a new creation, saying:

> "This will be written for the generation to come, that a people yet to be created may praise the LORD." (Ps. 102:18)

That means the end of the Old Creation had to be in view in order for God to create a new people. Otherwise, as Don Preston argued in a Facebook post on the *"As It Is Written"* page, God must destroy the church, i.e. the current "new creation" (2 Cor. 5:17) to fulfill this text.

Let me repeat that. If Psalms 102:18-26 is a reference to the material creation, then God has to destroy the present new covenant church in order to create a new people (who are as of now yet to be created) that may praise him. That is a horrible interpretation. It shows how far these literal futurists' claims destroy the integrity of the Scriptures and create doctrines that even they cannot with good conscience uphold.

Paul wrote to the Corinthians saying they were the generation of which David spoke. "Now all these things happened to them as examples, and they were written for our admonition, upon whom the ends [tele] of the ages have come." Paul said the end of the ages had come upon their generation. They, however, had died to the old age and were being translated into and transformed by the new creation (2 Cor. 5:17; Col. 1:18; Rev. 3:14).

This interpretation harmonizes and creates unity between the passing of the heaven and earth of Hebrews 1:10-12 and Hebrews 12:25-27 as one and the same, occurring in the first century. It cannot be denied that the Old Covenant heaven and earth under Torah was already **"being shaken"** when the epistle to the Hebrews was written.

"Whose voice then shook the earth; but now He has promised, saying, "Yet once more I shake not only the earth, but also heaven. Now this, Yet once more,' indicates the removal of those things that are being shaken, as of things that are made, that the things which cannot be shaken may remain."

The phrase **"things that are made"** is an ellipsis for **"being made with hands"**. The contrast is clearly with the kingdom of verse 28, which as noted above in Daniel 2:34, 44-45, is the kingdom or stone cut from the mountain **"without hands"**.

The quote above is taken from Haggai 2:6, who adds the words,

"Once more (it is a little while) I will shake heaven and earth, the sea and dry land."

Paul brings both this prophecy and Habakkuk 2:3 together to identify the appointed time of the vision as that which will not delay, Heb. 10:37. In the text before us, he uses the word, **"now"** to indicate the **present action** of the text.

In other words, "now" is the appointed time of Haggai and Habakkuk's vision. Now, means at the time of Paul's writing of Hebrews. For other references of "now" in Paul's eschatological writings, See 2 Cor. 6:2, Rom. 8:18; 13:11-12. Therefore, when he writes, "Whose voice then shook the earth; but now He has promised, saying, "Yet one more I shake not only the earth, but also heaven," he is contrasting what occurred at Sinai with what soon would happen to that old age of Judaism.

Summary of Hebrews 1:10-12

In the light of the context, the word world in Hebrews 1:12 is *ages* meaning the Jewish age. Paul identified the ages as the time of the *offering of Israel's sacrifices* through the **Levitical priesthood**, Heb. 9:26a. He stated that Jesus died in the **"consummation of the ages"** by offering himself as a sacrifice for sins (Heb. 9:26b). This places the *"purging of our sins"* and the *"ages" of Hebrews 1:2* in the same "sacrificial context". The phrase "kat arche" and "apo katabole comos" have been clearly demonstrated to be a contrast of the beginning of the Jewish age and the **consummation of that same age in which Jesus died.** For a more detailed study of the relationship of the two ages, see the video review of Drew Leonard on the subject.[14]

Paul taught that the consummation of the age had come upon "his own" generation, i.e. within the first century. The context of Ps. 102 is the passing of the Old Covenant people of God and the creation of the New Covenant people of God, less we end up destroying the New Covenant people or the church. The context of Psalm 102:18, 25, 26, Hebrews 1 and the entire epistle to the Hebrews is a contrast between the Old Covenant heaven and earth and the New Covenant heaven and earth. Verses 1:10-12 should be read and understood in that light.

---

[14] https://www.youtube.com/watch?v=kuy8nTxuTxQ&t

Chapter 10:
The Material Creation and the New Covenant

Additionally, in my viewpoint, God contrasts another creation with his new covenant creation, i.e. the physical universe and the heavenly bodies.

Psalm 89:34-37

We examined God's promise in Genesis 8:21-22 where He promised never again to destroy the world as He had done although man's heart was evil from his youth. God promised to be merciful to His creation and assured them that the earth and continual harvests, seedtime, winter, summer, and day and night would not cease.

Some believe that God speaks of the method of destruction. In other words, they reason that God destroyed the world of Noah's day by a flood but will destroy the material universe at some future time by fire. We do admit that 2 Peter chapter 3 has language which on the surface sounds as though God speaks of a fiery conflagration of the universe. But, the language, if taken literally, would contradict other plain teachings of the Bible as are demonstrated in this writing. Let's consider what David said about the new covenant and the reign of Christ.

> "My covenant I will not break, nor alter the word that has gone out of My lips. Once I have sworn by My holiness; I will not lie to David: His see shall endure forever, And his throne as the sun before Me; It shall be established forever like the moon, even like the faithful witness in the sky." (Psalm 89:34-37)

Now, if there is one veritable truth of the Bible, it is that Christ's reign is eternal and continues forever without end.

> "Of the increase of His government and peace there will be no end, to order it with judgment and justice from that time forward, even forever." (Isa. 9:7) See also Dan. 2:44; Lk. 1:32-33).

In the previous section, we saw that the Lord, i.e. and his kingdom is that which remains and cannot be shaken as compared to the Old Covenant heaven and earth. What assurance does God give that Christ's kingdom will never end? He says that Christ's kingdom is as permanent as the sun and the moon before Him.

God said he would not lie to David, but that his seed would remain forever and His throne as the sun and be established forever as the moon. What then is God telling us about the material physical creation? He says it is as permanent as the kingdom of Christ. But the kingdom of Christ has no end. Therefore, the sun and moon have no end. How much more clear could the Bible be that God will never destroy the material creation?

> The Kingdom of Christ has no end.
> The kingdom of Christ is as permanently enduring as the sun and moon.
> Therefore, the sun and moon have no end.

Is it not then a gross error to teach that God will one day destroy the universe? If he destroys the heavens, the earth and all its physical elements, would that not also mean the eternal non-ending kingdom of Christ must come to an end? If not, why not?

Psalms 72:5

They shall fear You, as long as the sun and moon endure throughout all generations."

Psalms. 72:7

In His days the righteous shall flourish, and abundance of peace, until the moon is no more.

Psalms 72:17

His name shall endure forever; His name shall continue as long as the sun. And men shall be blessed in Him. All nations shall call Him blessed.

Psalms 93:1

The LORD reigns, He is clothed with majesty, The LORD is clothed, He has girded Himself with strength. Surely the world is established, so that it cannot be moved.

Psalms 96:10

Say among the nations, "The LORD reigns; The world also is firmly established, It shall not be moved; He shall judge the peoples righteously.

Psalms 104:5

You who laid the foundations of the earth, so that it should not be moved.

Psalms 125:1

Those who trust in the LORD are like Mount Zon, which cannot be moved, but abides forever. As the mountains surround Jerusalem, so the LORD surrounds His people from this time forth and forever.

Psalms 148

Let them praise the name of the Lord, for He commanded and they were created. He also established them forever and ever; He made a decree which shall not pass away."

This is the Psalm recognized throughout Christianity as a doxology of praise to God by every created thing. God begins this praise with the heavens, and the sun, moon and stars of light. Observe what He has to say about them.

Where did God make this decree? Is that not the promise made to Noah that seedtime, harvest, winter and summer and day and night shall not cease while earth remains. Can God's Covenant with David be Broken? Could God have made that promise with the Old Covenant? Will Christ's kingdom continue as long as the Old Covenant? That would be a very short reign on the throne.

And the word of the Lord came to Jeremiah, saying, Thus says the Lord; if you can break My covenant with the day and My covenant with the night, so that there will not be day and night in their season, then My covenant may also be broken with David My servant, so that he shall not have a son to reign on his throne, and with the Levites, the priests, My ministers. As the host of heaven cannot be numbered, nor the sand of the sea measured, so will I multiply the descendants of David My servant and the Levites who minister to Me.' (Jeremiah 33:19-22)

This passage is critical to the study of the continuation of the physical universe, i.e. the sun, moon and stars. God based His promise of an everlasting, unbreakable covenant with David on the ever-enduring covenant of the day and night. This unmistakably alludes to Genesis 8:22. So goes the one, so goes the other. If God can break his covenant with David so that Christ does not reign on the throne, then he can break His covenant that day and night shall not cease. David, through the Spirit, comments on whether God could do such a thing.

"The Lord has sworn and will not relent, you are a priest forever according to the order of Melchizedek." (Ps. 110:4)

We are well aware that Christ would be a priest on his throne, (Psa. 110:1-2; Zech. 6:12-13). What's notable here is God's promise that he would not relent. He would not renege on the promise. He would not break his covenant to place Christ on David's throne. Even in the midst of enemy opposition, God said he would laugh at the attempt of the enemies to thwart his promise.

"He who sits in the heavens shall laugh; The Lord shall hold them in derision. Then He shall speak to them in His wrath, and distress them in His deep displeasure; Yet I have set My King on my holy hill of Zion." I will declare the decree; The Lord has said to Me, You are my Son, today I have begotten you. Ask of Me, and I will give you the nations for your inheritance, and the ends of the earth for your possession." (Psa. 2:4-8)

Peter affirmed that God swore by oath to David that Christ would sit on his throne. Thus, God swore He would not break his covenant.

Therefore, being a prophet and knowing that God had sworn with an oath to him that of the fruit of his body, according to the flesh He would raise up the Christ to sit on his throne…" (Acts 2:30-35).

As with the promise of Abraham (in actuality the same promise), God, unable to swear by one greater, swore by Himself. Thus, His oath is immutable. Paul affirms that God's covenant promise to David is forever and ever.

> "But to the Son He says; Your throne, O God, is forever and ever; a scepter of righteousness is the scepter of your kingdom." (Heb. 1:8)

The Levites

What of the Levites in the text? Does this not affirm that God speaks of the Old Covenant verses the New? Is He affirming the continuation of the *natural* seed of Israel and the perpetuity of the Old Covenant temple rituals? Is this a promise that the Levitical priesthood will be reestablished? This answer is no to all. The promise of the Levites points to the spiritual nature of the New Covenant and the priests who serve therein. Isaiah, speaking of the glory of the heavenly Zion and New covenant creation that God would make says when the time arrived His glory would be declared among the Gentiles. This speaks of the time the gospel message goes out from the apostles in the first century. At that time, God says:,

> "And I will take some of them for priests and Levites, says the Lord. For as the new heavens and the new earth which I will make shall remain before Me, says the Lord, so shall your descendants and your name remain." (Isa. 66:21-22)

Therefore, the "priests and Levites" mentioned here are figurative descriptions of the priests of the New Covenant heavens and earth that God created through Christ. See 1 Pet. 1:5, 9, and Rev. 1:6. Although this is true, God did in fact take some of the Levites of that Old Covenant system to serve in the new covenant creation temple."

> "Then the word of God spread and the number of the disciples multiplied greatly in Jerusalem, and a great many of the priests were obedient to the faith." (Acts 6:7)

This text clearly shows that Levites did in fact minister to God in the new creation. That God speaks of the conversion of not only Levites but multitudes of believers is evident from Jeremiah 33:20-22.

"Thus says the LORD: 'If you can break My covenant with the day and My covenant with the night, so that there will not be day and night in their season, Then My covenant may also be broken with David My servant, so that he shall not have a son to reign on his throne, and with the Levites, the priests, My ministers. As the host of heaven cannot be numbered, nor the sand of the sea measured, so will I multiply the descendants of David my servant and the Levites who minister to Me.'"

In the New covenant, all would become priests, both those formerly of the Levitical order as well as all the twelve tribes and the Gentiles. Through Christ all are priests, 1 Peter 2:5-6; Rev. 1:5-6, 5:10, 20:4-6. God's desire from the beginning was that Israel be a nation of priests, Ex. 19:5-6. This literally became true in the New Covenant.

Restoration from Babylonian Captivity in 536 B.C.

Some today are now teaching that because Isaiah 66:21-22 and Jeremiah 33:20-22 teach that the Levites would serve in the temple of the new heavens and earth, that the new heavens and earth was fulfilled in second temple Judaism during the time of the return from Babylonian captivity. The obvious reason for this interpretation is to circumvent and evade the force of the everlasting, perpetual reign of Christ on the throne in the kingdom of God. It also seeks to destroy the efficacy of the New Covenant claiming it began in the time of the return of the captives from Babylon.

1. Some claim the new covenant was established during the time of the return of the captives from Babylon in 536 B.C. Bill Lockwood and Stephen Wiggins advanced this view during the early to mid-nineties when we met them in debate. Today, other groups such as Israel only are now advancing this view.[15] The ratification of a covenant requires the shedding of blood. We understand this from the ratification of the covenant of Moses. To ratify means to make it official, accept, validate, authorize, etc. We see this in Heb. 9:18-22:

15

18) "Therefore not even the first covenant was dedicated without blood. 19) For when Moses had spoken every precept to all the people according to the law, he took the blood of calves and goats, with water, scarlet wool, and hyssop, and sprinkled both the book itself and all the people, 20) saying, 'This is the blood of the covenant which God has commanded you." 21) Then likewise he sprinkled with blood both the tabernacle and all the vessels of the ministry. 22) And according to the law almost all things are purified with blood, and without shedding of blood there is no remission."

2. This being true for the first covenant made with Moses, how much more so was it true for the new covenant? The shedding of animals' blood means those animals had to give their lives for the old covenant. That is what the "shedding of blood means", i.e. the giving of life. In like manner death was necessary for the ratification of the New Covenant. Recently, an outspoken opponent of Covenant Eschatology advocated that the new covenant began under Zerubbabel, governor of Judah? How can this be? Zerubbabel did not die for the new covenant. Nor did the Old Covenant end during the time of his government in Israel. Yet, the Bible teaches that the enactment of a testament required the death of the testator.

15) And for this reason He is the Mediator of the new covenant, by means of death, for the redemption of the transgression under the first covenant, that those who are called may receive the promise of eternal inheritance. 16) For where there is a testament, there must also of necessity be the death of the testator. 17) For a testament is in force after men are dead, since it has no power at all while the testator lives."

If the new covenant was established under Zerubbabel in the 5th century B.C. then it was established without a Mediator.

For there is one Mediator between God and men, the Man Christ Jesus. (1 Tim. 2:5).

Secondly, Zerubbabel did not enact a covenant that could take away sins. He continued to practice the laws of the old covenant. Not one jot or tittle of that law could pass till all were fulfilled. That means heaven and earth would have had to pass in Zerubbabel's time. Since Zerubbabel was himself a sinner, his blood could not atone for sin.

The net result of this claim for the inauguration of the new covenant in the time of Zerubbabel means that Jesus died to establish yet another new covenant, that is, if the new covenant claimed to be established in the time of Zerubbabel is not the same covenant of which we read about in the new testament. Therefore, we have two new covenants. If not, then when Jesus said, "For this is my blood of the new testament which is shed for many for the remission of sins, it would mean he shed His blood on the cross before he ever came to dwell with men on earth! We'll say more on Zerubbabel later.

3. Another reason the establishment of the new covenant is given for the time of the restoration of the captives from Babylon is the claim that the governor of Judah is called the Branch in the prophecy of Isaiah 11:1. One author asserted that Jesus Christ is not the root and offspring of Jesse, hence the descendant of David in the prophecy. He stated rather, it referred to Zerubbabel. Let's take note of the text.

1) "There shall come forth a Rod from the stem of Jesse, and a Branch shall grow out of his roots. The Spirit of the LORD shall rest upon Him, The Spirit of wisdom and understanding, The Spirit of counsel and might, the Spirit of knowledge and of the fear of the LORD. 3) His delight is in the fear of the LORD, and He shall not judge by the sight of His eyes, nor decide by the hearing of His ears; 4) But with righteousness He shall judge the poor, and decide with equity for the meek of the earth; He shall strike the earth with the rod of His mouth, and with the breath of His lips He shall save the wicked. Righteousness shall be the belt of His waist." (Isaiah 11:1-4)

First, before we address the Branch, let us note the surrounding context. The time for the event in this text is judgment. See in verses 3 and 4. Zerubbabel lived after a judgment had already occurred upon Israel. God had judged them for their sins, placed them under bondage for 70 years, and then released them to return to their land. His was not a time of judgment.

Secondly, it was said that the Branch cannot be a reference to Christ because His name will be called the Lord, and Christ is already the Lord. The argument was made from Isaiah 9:6-7, a text we will examine later, but the point would apply here also. This is a very specious argument. First, Yahweh called Christ Lord. "The Lord said to my Lord, 'Sit at My right hand, till I make Your enemies Your footstool.'" Jesus applied this very prophecy to Himself when the Pharisees attempted to deny His deity. "While the Pharisees were gathered together, Jesus asked them, saying, "what do you think about the Christ? Whose Son is He?" They said to Him, "The Son of David." He said to them, 'How then does David in the Spirit call Him 'Lord,' saying: 'The LORD said to My Lord, 'Sit at My right hand, Till I make Your Enemies Your footstool'?" If David then calls Him 'Lord,' how is He his Son?" (Matt. 22:41-46)

In addition, when Jesus was born, Joseph was told to call His name JESUS, for He will save His people from their sins. (Matt. 1:21). If to call him Lord means he was not Lord, then to call the Lord Jesus means he was not Jesus! How ridiculous and absurd! Verse 23 quotes from Isaiah 7:15 where Jesus' name would be called "Immanuel, which is translated, 'God with Us'". Since Jesus would be called God with us does this mean he was not God? These are the arguments of a desperate man trying to save a defeated theory.

4. Isaiah first mentions the Branch in the context of judgment in Isaiah 4:2-6. "In that day the Branch of the LORD shall be beautiful and glorious; and the fruit of the earth shall be excellent and appealing for those of Israel who have escaped. 3) And it shall come to pass that he who is left in Zion and remains in Jerusalem will be called holy—every one who is recorded among the living in Jerusalem. 4) When the Lord has washed away the filth of the daughters of Zion, and purged the blood of Jerusalem from her midst, by the spirit of judgment and by the spirit of burning. 5) then the Lord will create above every dwelling place of Mount Zion and above her assemblies, a cloud and smoke by day and the shining of a flaming fire by night. For over all the glory there will be a covering. 6) And there will be a tabernacle for shade in the daytime from the heat, for a place of refuge, and for a shelter from storm and rain."

This brief text contains every element of the end times summed in a succinct context.

- The Branch would be beautiful and glorified. This is a reference to Christ's coronation as king.

- He saves the remnant, i.e. those who escaped, recording their names in the "book of life."

- He keeps his covenant to Israel in removing their sins. Compare Isaiah 59:20-21, Rom. 11:27; Jer. 31:31-34; Heb. 8:6-12; 10:16.

- He purges the guilt for the shedding of innocent blood in Jerusalem.

- He delivers the people through the second exodus protecting them in the day through a cloudy pillar and a flame of fire by night. This allusion to the second exodus cannot be missed. It is the same context of Isaiah 11, and the very theme of the entire New Testament. However, the book of Hebrews focuses on the second Exodus in unmistakable language, Heb. 3:7-4:9.

- At the completion of their "wilderness wandering through forty years of persecution and trial, the Branch shelters them from the heat giving them refuge in the heavenly tabernacle. See 2 Cor. 5:1-10, Eph. 2:19-22; 1 Pet. 2:5-6; Heb. 9:8-23, Rev. 21:3-4.

5. The context of judgment for the Branch begins in Isaiah 2:2-4 which speaks of the last days when the Lord would build the house of God through establishing a new covenant. "Last days" is from the Hebrew "achyrith" and means, not the middle of the days, but the extremity, or last of the days. Isaiah does not speak of the beginning nor of the mid-point of Israel's history but of the terminal generation.

2) Now it shall come to pass in the latter days that the mountain of the LORD's house shall be established on the top of the mountains, and shall be exalted above the hills; and all nations shall flow to it. 3) Many people shall come and

say, Come, and let us go up to the mountain of the LORD, to the house of the God of Jacob; He will teach us His ways, and we shall walk in His paths." For out of Zion shall go forth the law, and the word of the LORD from Jerusalem. 4) He shall judge between the nations, and rebuke many people; They shall be their swords into plowshares, and their speaks into pruning hooks; Nation shall not lift up sword against nations, neither shall they learn war anymore."

Isaiah's prophecy focuses on the last days. The mountain of the Lord is the kingdom of God established in the time of the Messiah, Dan. 2:44,45, 7:15-28, 12:13. All Daniel's prophecies of the last days occurred during the time of the Roman Empire. Where was Rome during the 5th century B.C.? It certainly could not be the historical and prophetic time frame for Zerubbabel who expired years before the time of the Roman Empire.

In those days the nations would be gathered together in one, as many as obeyed the word of God. See Matthew 24:31, Matt. 8:11-12; Eph. 1:10. In the New Testament this is called the "fullness of times". It is the time in which Christ came born of a woman, made under the Law (Gal. 4:4). During his ministry he preached that the time was fulfilled and that the kingdom of heaven had drawn near. (Mk. 1:14-15) At no previous time in history had the prophets spoke of the kingdom being near. To the contrary, they formerly prophesied of things afar off.

The judgment theme of chapter two extends through verses 10-11. Those who flee the judgment look for shelter in the rocks and dust. Jesus applied this language to Israel showing that when the Romans sacked the city, they would cry out to the rocks and seek to hide in caves. "But Jesus, turning to them, said,

"Daughters of Jerusalem, do not weep for Me, but weep for yourselves and for your children. 29) For indeed the days are coming in which they will say, 'Blessed are the barren, wombs that never bore, and breasts which never nursed!' 30) Then they will begin to say to the mountains, 'Fall on us!' and to the hills, 'Cover us!'" (Luke 23:28-30)

Again in Revelation, John refers to Isaiah's prophecy spoken by Christ.

"And the kings of the earth, the great men, the rich en, the commanders, the mighty men, every slave and every free man, hid themselves in the caves and in the rocks of the mountains, and said to the mountains and rocks, 'Fall on us and hides us from the face of Him who sits on the throne and from the wrath of the Lamb! For the great day of His wrath has come, and who is able to stand?" (Rev. 6:15-17)

Compare these words with another verse from Isaiah 2:19-21.

"They shall go into the holes of the rocks, and into the caves of the earth, from the terror of the LORD and the glory of His majesty, when He arises to shake the earth mightily. In that day a man will cast away his idols of silver and his idols of gold, which they made, each for himself to worship, to the moles and bats, 21) to go into the clefts of the rocks, and into the crags of the rugged rocks from the terror of the LORD and the glory of His majesty, when he arises to shake the earth mightily."

6. Having developed the judgment framework of the "Branch" in Isaiah 4, we now return to Isaiah 11.

"There shall come forth a Rod from the stem of Jesse, and a Branch shall grow out of his roots." At this time the Gentiles would be gathered. "And in that day there shall be a Root of Jesse, who shall stand as a Banner to the people; For the Gentiles shall seek Him and His resting place shall be glorious. (Is. 11:1, 10).

Twice in referring to the Branch, Isaiah alludes to the exodus. We noticed above in chapter 4 when speaking of the cloud and pillar of fire, culminating in the tabernacle of God, and here with the "resting place". This is why we say that Isaiah speaks of the time of the second exodus. It also is the time of the outpouring of the Spirit upon Christ. Compare Isaiah 11:2, 61:1, John 1:32.

One of the stronger evidences for the application of Isaiah 11 to the last days apostolic ministry is Paul's citation of Isaiah 11:10 in Romans 15. His approach to the text is noteworthy. He begins with a series of prophecies from the Old Covenant which speak of the Gentiles applying all of them to the current apostolic ministry in the first century.

Now I say that Jesus Christ has become a servant to the circumcision for the truth of God to confirm the promises made to the fathers, [9] and that the

Gentiles might glorify God for His mercy, as it is written: 'For this reason I will confess to You among the Gentiles, and sing to Your name.' [10] And again he says: 'Rejoice, O Gentiles, with His people!' [11] And again: 'Praise the LORD, all you Gentiles!, Laud Him, All you peoples!'

Paul says it is Jesus Christ who became the servant of God to confirm the promises made to the fathers. His proofs are quoted from 2 Samuel 22:50 and Psalm 18:49. David has conquered Goliath and the Philistines. He and his men had killed four of the giant's descendants. He wrote the song of 2 Samuel 22, also recorded in Psalm 18:49, that he would sing praises among the peoples, i.e. in the presence of the Gentiles. Paul cites the text to show once again, Jesus' victory merited a song of praise in the midst of Gentiles.

The next quote from Deuteronomy clearly refers to the last days. Moses speaks to Israel about their end citing specifically the terminal perverse and crooked generation. John, the Baptist, (Matt. 3:7, Christ, (Matt. 12:38-45; 16:1-4; 23:32-37) and the apostles' Peter (Acts 2:40) and Paul, (Phil. 2:15) and John (Rev. 18:20-24, spoke of this wicked generation. Others N.T. writers alluded to them. See Jude. Moses connects the rejoicing of the Gentiles, with His people (Israel). Thus, they are not the same. It is at that time when God would avenge the blood of His servants. We have listed a sufficient number of texts to support this point. Seeing then all the prophecies refer to the time of God's people rejoicing that God has taken vengeance on His enemies in the last days, there can be no doubt for the time and application of Isaiah 11:10 with the Branch.

"And again, Isaiah says: 'There shall be a root of Jesse; and He who shall rise to reign over the Gentiles, In Him the Gentiles shall hope.' (Rom. 15:10).

The evidence for the last days application overwhelmingly favors Jesus Christ in the fullness of time, versus Zerubbabel.

7. Now that we have established Isaiah 11:1, 10 in that judgment context of God's vengeance, we now look at Zechariah chapter

3. It is asserted that Zerubbabel is the Branch of Zechariah chapters 3:8 and 6:12-13. Again, the whole intent of that argumentation is to remove Christ from the throne of Isaiah 9:6-7, eliminate the everlasting kingdom which has no end, and finally to make Zerubbabel the founder of the new covenant in the time of Jeremiah. It doesn't work.

Joshua, the high priest, represented himself and all Israel. God refused to allow Satan to condemn them even though their garments were defiled by sin. The Angel of God ordered the filthy garments to be taken away and new clothing and a clean turban or mitre given to Joshua. It is to Joshua that the Lord gave the command to walk in his ways and judge his house. Although Zerubbabel was the governor of the land, he did not have authority over the high priest to govern the house of God. Joshua and the company of priests would walk before the priestly chambers and among the priests, 3:2-7. Then God tells Joshua, the high priest, thus specifically identifying him both by name and official title, that he and his companions were a wondrous sign; because he was bringing forth His Servant the BRANCH.

8. **Jeremiah 31:35**

"Thus says the Lord, who gives the sun for a light by day, the ordinances of the moon for a light by night, who disturbs the sea, and its waves roar (The Lord of Hosts is his name): If those ordinances depart from before Me, says the Lord, then the seed of Israel shall also cease from being a nation before me forever." Thus says the Lord: If heaven above can be measured, and the foundations of the earth searched out beneath, I will also cast off all the seed of Israel for all they have done, says the Lord."

For example, when God speaks of the New Covenant, (Jer. 31:31f) he references these heavenly luminaries, i.e. the material creation of heaven and earth and repeats the covenant he made with Noah:

"While the earth remains, seedtime and harvest, winter and summer, and day and night shall not cease." (Gen. 8:22)

These words imply the material creation will not cease. Even though man's heart was evil from his youth after the flood, God said he would never again bring a catastrophe on the earth as he had done, (v. 21). Now remember, in the text from Psalms 89:36 that God said the seed of David would endure forever. Christ is the Seed of David. *"Concerning His Son Jesus Christ our Lord, who was born of the seed of David according to the flesh." (Rom. 1:4)*

But what of the people of God, namely, Christians? They too are the seed of David? Why? It's because God only has one seed. Those who belong to God through Christ are but "one seed" through Him. That is precisely the point Paul makes in Galatians 3:16.

> "Now to Abraham and his Seed were the promises made. He does not say, 'And to seeds,' as of many, but as of one, 'And to your Seed,' who is Christ."

Therefore, God's seed was not the entirety of fleshly Israel, (Rom. 2:28-29; 9:6-8) but singularly of Jesus Christ, who was raised from the dead in the realm of the Spirit, (1 Pet. 3:18(according to the power of Holiness through the Spirit, (Rom. 1:4).

However, it is through man entering a relationship with Christ that He becomes "one" not many by being joined to Christ. As Paul spoke of Marriage in Ephesians 5, he said that he spoke of a mystery involving Christ, i.e. that when believers are joined to Christ, they become one body, just like a husband and bride become one. Paul describes this process of becoming one with Christ as follows:

> "For you are all sons of God through faith in Christ Jesus. For as many of you as were baptized into Christ have put on Christ. There is neither Jew nor Greek, there is neither slave nor free, there is neither male nor female; for you are all one in Christ Jesus. And if you are Christ's then you are Abraham's seed, and heirs according to the promise." (Gal. 3:26-29)

Thus, Paul says those in Christ, are all one [seed]. Therefore, Christ is the Seed of Israel and all who are in him make up that one Seed. Now if God says he would not cast off the seed of Israel, he therefore in my judgment is speaking of the seed of Christ and the church as one united in covenant as man and wife. They are one. Since God promised that He would not lie to David and that his kingdom would remain forever, we see this as Christ upon the throne of David ruling without end. It is God's promise to never cast off Israel, but in what manner? If God were to cast off the seed, he must cast of the Messiah. This could never be for the kingdom of Christ is without end.

Paul raises the question of God casting off his people Israel in consideration of the New Covenant gospel preached to Israel. The casting away of Israel is Paul's very point in Romans 11:1, where he asks,

"Has God cast away his people whom he foreknew? Certainly not! For I also am an Israelite, of the seed of Abraham, of the tribe of Benjamin."

Another way of answering that question could have been, Certainly not! For the sun, moon and stars above yet shine. However, that would not have been germane to Paul's point of proving that he and other Jews were at that time the living proof. In so doing, he makes both arguments in one.

In addition, if the creation of Genesis 8:22 and the "day and night" refer to elements of the Old Covenant then this text would clearly contradict those above where God promised to destroy the Old Covenant world, as in Hebrews, Psalms and Isaiah. In other words, if these verses represent the Old Covenant heaven and earth which would perish then: (1) there is a direct contradiction between Heb. 1:10-12 and Gen. 8:22; Psa. 89:34-37 and Jer. 31:35; 33:20). (2) If on the other hand it is the Old Covenant world which does not perish hence remains, what then would be the comparison with the Lord, i.e. the New Covenant heaven and earth?

Likewise, since they form the basis of the continuation of the new heaven and earth, i.e. the surety and guarantee of that continuity, they likewise cannot be the same as the new heavens and earth. Such reasoning would be circular indeed to say the New Covenant remains because the New Covenant remains! Hence, we have a separate physical creation and likewise seasons, planting time, weather, and "day and night" essential for existence of agriculture and biological life. I barely escaped science, so I'm not about to enter that discussion but I read somewhere that sunlight is essential to plant growth. Not once did my science book say the Old Covenant was necessary to raising crops.

Jeremiah said as long as the ordinances of the sun, moon and stars continue, the seed of Israel would continue as a nation, (which I take to be the New Covenant redeemed nation (the remnant inclusive of the northern tribes and the Gentiles, thus "all Israel," (Rom. 11:26) per the context. If they refer to the Old Covenant nation, then should not the celestial bodies of the sun, moon and stars have dropped from the sky in 70 A.D.? I hesitate to say that we are growing our crops by virtue of the New Covenant sunlight, except as God is the ultimate cause, but the point should be clear.

That I May Plant the Heavens – Isaiah 51:16

"That I May Plant the Heavens" of Isaiah 51:16, is debated as to its application. Is it Genesis One or the kingdom? The inquiries around this text offer three possible solutions for interpretation. Some believe that it refers historically to Genesis 1:1, but not to a physical creation. Rather, they see it as the covenantal creation of Israel, predating Sinai. (See Beyond Creation Science by Jeffrey Vaughn and Tim Martin). Others offer Sinai at the giving of the Law. Yet another group believes it refers to the kingdom age.

> "And I have put my words in your mouth; I have covered you with the shadow of My hand, that I may plant the heavens, lay the foundations of the earth, and say to Zion, 'You are my people.'" (Isa. 51:16)

Adam Clarke is very sparse in his comments on the text. He offers justification for what we wrote above saying the text is very obscure. That doesn't help much! Young, a bit more generous acknowledges that the words are reminiscent of Sinai. However, he sees a future perspective in the second half of the verse. "Yet the second half of the verse seems to suggest that the work therein described is to be carried out by those in whose mouth God has placed His words. They are to plant the heavens and found the earth. God places His words in their mouth that thereby the heavens and earth may be founded."[16]

---

[16] Edward Young, The New International Commentary on the Old Testament, The Book of Isaiah Vol. I, p 318

Young further adds that the more likely view is that the prophecy refers to the work of the Servant of God, i.e. the Messiah. He reasons that the planting of the heavens and founding of the earth is not generally the work of Isaiah and the prophets. While Israel may be a consideration, it could only be representative of the one Seed through whom Israel is determined, i.e. the Lord Jesus Christ. Young concludes:

> "Yet in light of the nature of the work to be accomplished, it seems best to regard the One in whose mouth God places His words as the Messiah Himself, the One who is to plant the heavens and found the earth and bring a message of comfort to Zion."

God says he would put the words into the Messiah's mouth. This is affirmed both by Deuteronomy 18:18-19 and John 14:10; 16:13. Now, since the heavens and earth were already created when Isaiah wrote, he could not be speaking of the material creation. Further, he could not be speaking of Sinai for the same reason. It currently ran its course as he spoke.

The language of Isaiah is clearly future tense as expressed in the LXX (Septuagint or Greek translation of the Old Testament.

> (**I will** put my words into thy mouth, and **I will** shelter thee under the shadow of mine hand, with which I fixed the sky, and founded the earth; and the Lord shall say to Sion, Thou are my people." (Emp. Mine).

In this text observe that God affirms that the Messiah would be sheltered under the shadow of his hand with which he "fixed" the sky. This is an allusion to the permanence of the material creation. This further confirms that he speaks of a future creation. This text is parallel to Isaiah 65:17 where God says he would make a new creation and a new people. Only there he uses Jerusalem, in the place of Zion as the place of the creation.

In previous verses, God had just spoken of the passing of the Old Covenant heaven and earth comparing it with the salvation which comes through the Messiah which would not be abolished. (Isa. 51:6) Thus, the heavens and earth God would create per Isaiah 51:16 would not be abolished. Let me sum up by saying we have shown that the words of Isaiah 51:16 refer not to Gen. 1:1 (material creation). We demonstrated it could not be the Old Covenant creation at Sinai, in that that creation would pass away, whereas the new heavens and earth God would create would remain. Since the material creation is "fixed" then it will not vanish away. Then it was the Old Covenant which passed away like smoke and vanishes like a garment. Therefore, the reference in Isaiah 51:16 speaks of the New Covenant creation under the Messiah and the New Israel or new people (Christians) who inhabit that new covenant world.

Isaiah 50:6-9

> "I gave my back to those who struck Me, and My cheeks to those who plucked out the beard; I did not hide My face from shame and spitting. For the Lord God will help Me; Therefore I will not be disgraced; Therefore I have set My face like a flint and I know that I will not be ashamed. He is near who justifies Me; who will contend with Me? Let us stand together. Who is My adversary? Let him come near Me. Surely the Lord God will help Me; who is he who will condemn Me? Indeed they will all grow old like a garment; The moth will eat them up."

This is another Messianic text. It portrays the Servant of God who suffers at the hands of adversaries. He is not moved because the shame is temporary. It lasts but a "moment." The text of Hebrews 12:2 captures the sentiment.

> "Looking unto Jesus, the author and finisher of our faith, who for the joy that was set before Him endured the cross, despising the shame, and has sat down at the right hand of the throne of God."

The cross, an agonizing moment of shame soon turned into victorious glory in Christ's resurrection and enthronement declared at His glorious return. Jesus trusted God as His help. Thus, his face was set forth like a flint. God was near him, standing at His side as a defense attorney to contend against every accusation or case brought against him.

Jesus' adversaries are said to grow old as a garment, an expression used of the slow decay or deterioration of a garment that is eaten up by a moth. Those who attempt to accuse him would grow old as a garment. The moth would eat them up as easily as they devour a garment.

Consider Hebrews 8:13 that speaks of the Old Covenant growing old and becoming outdated.

> "In that He says, A new covenant, He has made the first obsolete. Now what is becoming obsolete and growing old is ready to vanish away."

The Isaianic text depicts Israel in the time of Messiah. They attack him, then turn their attention to the saints. They, bring charge against Him and the saints until they are destroyed. The language is strikingly similar to that of Hebrews 8:13, in speaking of the Old Covenant As the Lord and the New Covenant world remain from generation to generation, the Old Covenant world and its people cease.

Isaiah 51:6-8

The imagery of the enemies of Christ wearing out as a garment and eaten by the moth is carried through the context of chapter 51. The focus now becomes the "heavens and earth," as the place of dwelling of those enemies.

> "Lift up your eyes to the heavens, and look on the earth beneath. For the heavens will vanish away like smoke, the earth will grow old like a garment, and those who dwell in it will die in like manner; but my salvation will be forever, and my righteousness will not be abolished." Listen to Me, you who know righteousness, you people whose heart is My law; Do not fear the reproach of men, nor be afraid of their insults. For the moth will earth them up like a garment, and the worm will eat them like wool; but My righteousness will be forever, and my salvation from generation to generation. (Isa. 51:6-8)

A one passage commentary on these verses is Matthew 24:35, the words quoted by Christ to express the meaning found here.

> "Heaven and earth shall pass away but My words will by no means pass away."

As in Isaiah, Jesus peaks of the Old Covenant world. He predicts it would pass in A.D. 70, in the destruction of Jerusalem. Yet, His world (righteousness or the gospel, Rom. 1:16-17; 1 Peter 1:24-25) would by no means pass away.

This means that the physical world must of necessity remain intact. How else could such words of Christ be fulfilled? His righteousness would never be abolished, but would endure forever. His salvation continues from generation to generation. Thus, as Jesus' enemies of the Old Covenant who resisted Him, refused to allow Him to reign over them and who opposed and condemned Him, faded away, the church remained.

"To Him be glory in the church by Christ Jesus to all generations, for ever and ever, Amen." (Eph. 3:21)

It is for this reason that John admonished the saints not to love the Old Covenant world, nor lust after it as the first generation lusted after Egypt. In each case, they were lusting for a return to bondage.

"Do not love the world or the things in the world, If anyone love the world, the love of the Father is not in Him...And the world is passing away, and the lust of it; but he who does the will of God abides forever." (1 Jn. 2:15-17)

Thus, John's message is clear when compared with Isaiah, 51:6-8; Matthew 24:35 and Hebrews 1:10-12. See the following chart.

Old Covenant World	New Covenant World
Heavens will vanish like smoke, Isa. 51:6a	My salvation will be forever, Isa. 51:6a
Earth will grow old in like manner. Isa. 51:6b	My righteousness will not be abolished, Isa. 51:6b
Those who dwell in it will die in like manner, Isa. 51:6c	My righteousness will be forever, Isa. 51:8a
The moth will eat them up like a garment, and the worm will eat them like wool, Isa. 51:8	My salvation is from generation to generation, Isa. 51:8b
Heaven and earth will pass away, Matt. 24:35a	My world will by no means pass away, Matt. 24:3b
You Lord in the beginning laid the foundations of the earth and the heavens are the works of your hands; They will perish, Heb. 1:10-11a.	But you [Lord] are the same, Heb. 1:12c

They will all grow old like a garment, Heb. 1:11b. Like a clock you will fold them up, and they will be changed. (Compare Isa. 50:9; 51:8)	Your years will not fail, He. 1:12d
Yet once more I shake not only heaven but also earth, Heb. 12:26	Things which cannot be shaken may remain, Heb. 12:27b
Indicates the removal of those things what are being shaken, Heb. 12:27a	We receiving a kingdom which cannot be shaken, Heb. 12:28
And the world is passing away, 1 John 2:15	But he who does the will of God abides forever. 1 Jn. 2:15b

The chart above shows how each passage respectively refers to either the Old Covenant or the New Covenant world. They are always contrasted as that which perishes, waxes old or is destroyed, versus that which remains or cannot be shaken. It is the Old Covenant world contrasted with the eternal kingdom of God.

I thought it also important to include another chart on the new people. In both Psalms 102 and Isaiah 51 and 65, God speaks of creating a new people. But, the new people are not created until the old world is destroyed, per the futurists. They reason that God is going to destroy the physical earth and afterwards create a new heaven and a new earth. God also taught he would create a new people. That means that Christians living today cannot be the "new people" God would create to dwell in the new heavens and earth! Thus, God must destroy all Christians with the earth in order to create a new people. This is how little thought has gone into the claim that God will one day destroy the physical universe. Consider the chart below that maps out the worlds of the futurists.

Confusing Worlds of Futurism

Old Covenant World/People	New Covenant People/ Material World	New People/New H & E
Ended at the cross, & End of O. C. World, 30AD	End at the end of the physical world (???)	Begin at the end of the physical world (???)
30 AD	Of old You laid the foundation of the earth, and the heavens are the work of your hands, They will perish…they will all grow old like a garment; like a cloak you will change them. (102:25-26)	This will be written for the generation to come, that a people yet to be created may praise the LORD, Psa. 102:18
30 AD	They all will grow old like a garment; the moth will eat them up (Isa. 50:9b)	The new people?
30 AD	Lift up your eyes to the heavens, and look on the earth beneath. For the heavens will vanish away like smoke, the earth will grow old like a garment. And those who dwell in it will die in like manner. (Isa. 51:6)	The new people?
30 AD	Heaven and earth shall pass away, Matt. 24:35; 2 Pet. 3:10; 1 Jn. 2:15-16; Heb. 1:10; 12:26-27; Rev. 6:12, 20:11; 21:1	That I may plant the heavens, Lay the foundations of the earth, and say to Zion, 'You are My people" (Isa. 51:16)
30AD	Former shall not be remembered or come to mind. Isa. 65:b	For behold, I create new heavens and a new earth; Isa. 65:a
30 AD		Create Jerusalem a rejoicing and her people a joy.

30 AD	All sinners, infants, children and elderly destroyed	Sinner, Infants, children elderly will live here.
30 AD	All houses, vineyards, fruit and trees destroyed	Houses, vineyards, fruit and trees will be here
30 AD	All works herein burned up	Here the elect long enjoy the work of their hands
30 AD	All births cease as no women survive	Women do not labor in vain and bring forth children without trouble
30 AD	All offspring destroyed	Offspring are descendants of the Lord, who have offspring, v. 23
30 AD	No calling upon the Lord and no answers	They call upon the Lord and are answered
30 AD	Wolf and the Lamb burned up (Jew & Gentile)	Wolf and the lamb feeds together (Jew & Gentile)
30 AD	Hurt in this world	No hurt in this holy mountain

The Worlds of the Bible

The Material Heaven and Earth Never Ends, Gen. 1:1; 8:21-22; Psa. 78:17; 89:34-37; Isa. 51:6, 8	
Old Covenant Heaven and Earth – Sinai to 70AD; Heb. 8:13; 2 Pet. 3:7-10	New Covenant Heaven & Earth – Jerusalem 70AD without End, Eph. 3:21; Heb. 12:28; 2 Pet. 3:13; 1 Jn. 2:17, continues as long as the Sun & Moon, i.e. as long as the material creation, Psa. 72:17; 89:34-37
Of old You laid the foundation of the earth, and the heavens are the work of your hands, They will perish…they will all grow old	This will be written for the generation to come, that a people yet to be created may praise the LORD, Psa. 102:18

like a garment; like a cloak you will change them. (102:25-26)

They all will grow old like a garment; the moth will eat them up (Isa. 50:9b)	Therefore if any man is in Christ, he is a new creation, 2 Cor. 5:17
Lift up your eyes to the heavens, and look on the earth beneath. For the heavens will vanish away like smoke, the earth will grow old like a garment. And those who dwell in it will die in like manner. (Isa. 51:6)	That I may plant the heavens, Lay the foundations of the earth, and say to Zion, 'You are My people" (Isa. 51:16)
Heaven and earth shall pass away, Matt. 24:35; 2 Pet. 3:10; 1 Jn. 2:15-16; Heb. 1:10; 12:26-27; Rev. 6:12, 20:11; 21:1	I create Jerusalem as a rejoicing and her people a joy. Isa 65:18

Chapter 11:
2 Peter 3

The sensible approach to understanding the meaning of 2 Peter 3 is to first understand Peter's teaching on the time of the end in the first epistle. Why do we say this? It's because Peter said that his second epistle was a reminder of the teachings found in the first letter.

> Beloved, I now write to you this second epistle (in both of which I stir up your pure minds by way of reminder), (2) that you may be mindful of the words which were spoken before by the holy prophets, and of the commandment of us, the apostles of the Lord and Savior, 2Pe 3:1-2

Secondly, another key to unlocking the meaning of 2 Peter three is to study the words of spoken by the Prophets and the apostles. Rather than resorting to what we learned in 9th grade science, church traditions or what we may have heard on the street or from popular doomsday evangelists on TV, these two methods commanded by Peter do serve the interpreter well. In other words, Peter has given us the process and methodology to most useful to understanding the chapter. On those two foundations, we offer our exposition.

The first epistle was written to Jews of the Dispersion or Diaspora who were in Asia Minor. (1:1) They are a very specific audience noted by the Old Testament Prophet, Hosea who spoke of their conversion in the last days.[17] (Hos. 1:10, 11, 1 Pet. 2:9, 10) Paul also confirms that the prophecies were being fulfilled in the New Testament era of the apostolic ministry, (Rom. 9:25, 26)

---

[17] For an excellent discussion see The Last Days Identified, by Don K. Preston with Contributions by John Anderson.

Peter addresses the Diaspora of **his day** and tells them that salvation was **ready** to be revealed in the **last time.** The word ready is significant. Its meaning is from Strong's Concordance:

> 2092 hétoimos (from heteos, "fitting") – ready because prepared; "standing by," ready to meet the opportunity (challenge) at hand; ready because the necessary preparations are done (or are sure to happen as needed).

As can be seen, this word means imminent, at hand, and suggests that all preparations were done for the specific event under discussion, namely, the eschatological salvation had come. The word is used for a bride who made all necessary preparations for the wedding. The language of Revelation 21:2 expresses the idea.

> Then I, John, saw the holy, New Jerusalem, coming down out of heaven from God, prepared as a bride adorned for her husband. And I heard a loud voice from heaven saying, 'Behold, the tabernacle of God is with men, and He will dwell with them, and they shall be His people. God Himself will be with them and be their God."

This is marriage language. It suggests the time for the eschatological wedding had come. In every instance, the marriage followed the destruction of the city and temple, Matt. 22:1-8, Matt. 24-25, Rev. 19:1-9 and 22:1-2.

Next, Peter discusses the "eschatological sufferings" or the "birth pangs" (Matt. 24:8, John 16:21-22, the first century disciples experienced prior to the Roman invasion of Jerusalem. This was the period during Jesus' going away and His Parousia, spoken of in John's gospel as "a little while", (John 14:19; 16:16-19). Paul said those were the sufferings of that present time, hence were not to be taken out of context for a protracted or centuries later time of fulfillment.

> For I consider that the sufferings of this present time are not worthy to be compared with the glory which shall [is about to, mello] be revealed in us. Rom 8:18

Peter likewise referred to these sufferings several times in His first epistle to speak of the fiery trial they were undergoing at that time.

> In this you greatly rejoice, though now for a little while, if need be, you have been grieved by various trials, (7) that the genuineness of your faith, being much

more precious than gold that perishes, though it is tested by fire, may be found to praise, honor, and glory at the revelation of Jesus Christ, (1Pe 1:6-7).

See also 3:13-16; 4:12.

It is in the context of these current and present sufferings that the end time was near. Peter uses the same word, "hetoimos" that he used in the first chapter v. 6.

> They will give an account to Him who is ready [Strong's 2092, hetoimos] to judge the living and the dead. (1Pe 4:5)

The use of "hetoimos" as in 1 Peter 1:6, means that all things were prepared and completed for the judgment of the living and the dead. In Acts 17:30, 24:14-15, 24, 26:22-23, and 2 Tim. 4:1, Paul used the word mello to express the idea that the judgment of the living and the dead was about to occur. Continuing his comments on the subject, Peter said the end had drawn near.

> But the end of all things is at hand; therefore be serious and watchful in your prayers. 1Pe 4:7

Due to the nearness of the end of all things, the first century saints were to be watchful in their prayers. Jesus spoke these words to the apostles during his sermon on the mount, exhorting them to watch, (Matt. 24:42-44, Mk. 13:35, 37, Lk. 21:36). Did Jesus deceive the first century saints to watch for something that was over 2000 years away? Such would have no relevance and meaning to a church then suffering fiery trials. They were to watch because He would come and put an end to those eschatological sufferings.

The next text Peter uses to set the stage for his second epistle is verse 17. He wrote that the time had come for "the" judgment to begin. The definite article is in the Greek text and can be checked with an interlinear[18]

> For the time has come for [the] judgment to begin at the house of God; and if it begins with us first, what will be the end of those who do not obey the gospel of God? (1Pe 4:17)

---

[18] English Version of the Bible with the corresponding Greek words in line with the English.

One final point Peter makes about the time of the end is found in Chapter 5 verse 1.

> The elders who are among you I exhort, I who am a fellow elder and a witness of the sufferings of Christ, and also a partaker of the glory that will [mello, is about to] be revealed:

This time, the apostle used the word of his fellow apostle Paul to speak of the nearness of Christ's coming in judgment. He says that Christ was "about to" be revealed. He used the present active participle, (mellouses) "being about to be revealed". In other words, Jesus' imminent coming was not reserved for a yet future time. He is not saying it will be imminent in the future, but rather, it was already imminent at that present time. The imminence was already a state of being. To sum up what Peter said in his first epistle, he taught that

- Salvation was ready [hetoimos] to be revealed in the last hour
- They were enduring the eschatological sufferings for "a little while" which would end at the revelation of Christ.
- The Lord was ready [hetoimos] to judge the living and the dead
- The end of all things had drawn near and,
- The time had come for the judgment to begin at the house of God.
- The glory of the Lord was being about to be revealed.

The above facts must be constantly kept in mind before proceeding to the second epistle. Now that we know what Peter taught about the end times in the first epistle, we are ready for 2 Peter 3, which Peter presents as a reminder of his earlier teaching.

Peter's Reminder 2 Peter 3:1

Now, Peter's reference to the first epistle and the subject of eschatology makes sense.

> Beloved, I now write to you this second epistle (in both of which I stir up your pure minds by way of reminder), (2) that you may be mindful of the words which were spoken before by the holy prophets, and of the commandment of us, the apostles of the Lord and Savior, (2Pe 3:1, 2)

Is there any doubt that Peter is referring to his first epistle? He said he stirred up their minds in both concerning his teaching of the last days. Would he teach two different doctrines on the end times from one epistle to the next? Would that not greatly confuse his audience? He specifically refers to the words of Christ. Jesus said he was about to come in judgment and reward each according to his works. He added that some who stood in His presence would not die until they saw him coming in His kingdom, (Matt. 16:27, 28). Futurists of all stripes are troubled by these verses. They have attempted to evade the force of Jesus' words that some of his disciples who were present with him would not die until he came in judgment in His kingdom. They have suggested the text meant the disciples would be reincarnated. How does the false notion of reincarnation prevent death? It doesn't. One would have to die, in order to be "re-incarnated" so that doesn't solve the problem at all. Further, would reincarnation eliminate dying again? Then, there is the question of what would the human be reincarnated as, a bird, a flea, or a rhinoceros? When does God reward animals in judgment?

Secondly, they claim that the transfiguration fulfills the text. Yet, not one person who makes this argument can prove that either the kingdom came at the time of the transfiguration or the judgment occurred at that time. If so, that would make that person a true "hyper-preterist" with no futurist cover under which to hide.

Thirdly, it is argued that the death in the text is not physical death, but the second death. This does not resolve the dilemma but makes it even worse. Here's why. Suppose we grant that the death in verse 28 is a reference to the second death. That only means that all the disciples would eventually suffer the second death! Does it sound better that some who stood with the Lord would not suffer the second death until he came in his kingdom? Doesn't that mean they would suffer the second death after he came? Such conclusion is unavoidable according to that premise. Did any disciple suffer the second death during the transfiguration? That is how ridiculous it is to make the death in verse 28 anything other than physical death. Jesus simply taught he would return before some of his disciples then living died. None are physically alive today. Therefore, we must admit that he came as he said he would. The only other option is to claim he was a liar or we have people walking the earth who are over 2000 years old! Jesus also taught the same in truth in Matthew 24:34. He taught that His generation would not pass away until all things were fulfilled.

In addition, we touched on words from the apostle Paul. See others in Rom. 13:11, 12, 1 Cor. 15:51, 52, 1 Thes. 4:15, 17, Phil. 4:5. James taught the Lord's coming had drawn near and the Judge stood at the door, Jas. 5:7-9. John said they knew they were in the last hour because the antichrist had come 1 Jn. 2:18,-19. In the book of Revelation he taught that the time was at hand, Rev. 1:1, had drawn near, 1:3, and that the events of the book were about to occur, 1:19. He repeated the same teaching in chapter 22:6, 10, 12, 20.

The Scoffers Come

knowing this first: that scoffers will come in the last days, walking according to their own lusts, (4) and saying, "Where is the promise of His coming? For since the fathers fell asleep, all things continue as they were from the beginning of creation." 2Pe 3:3-4

Perhaps one of the most unappreciated verses in 2 Peter 3 is this one. Peter mentions that Scoffers would come. He cites a text from the Old Testament Prophets.

Isa 28:22 Now therefore, do not be mockers, Lest your bonds be made strong; For I have heard from the Lord GOD of hosts, A destruction determined even upon the whole earth.

According to the NICNT,[19] the use of the term "scoffer" was the strongest O.T. term used to describe the wicked. This is a person who not only chooses the wrong way, but also mocks the right way.

To understand the significance of the presence of the Scoffers, we must know what Peter taught, and why they were mocking it. The reader is referred to the comments above showing that Peter clearly taught that Jesus' coming was ready to be revealed, was near and that

---

[19] New International Commentary of the New Testament

the time had come for the judgment to begin. This means, the scoffers had to reject this message of *imminence* and make mockery of it. Had Peter not taught that Jesus' coming was soon to occur, there would be no reason for the scoffers to come and to reject the message.

The scoffers came saying, "where is the promise of His coming? They no doubt were familiar with the teaching of the apostles that the coming of the Lord was near. However, on the other hand, they were saying, that coming is not near. It is not about to come. All things continue as they were from the beginning. If Peter had taught that Jesus' coming was not near but in the far distant future, he would certainly be in agreement with the scoffers! He would be scoffing against his own teaching and that of the prophets, the Lord and his fellow apostles.

When Stephen taught that Jesus would come and destroy the temple, the Jews charged him with blasphemy.

> They also set up false witnesses who said, "This man does not cease to speak blasphemous words against this holy place and the law; (14) for we have heard him say that this Jesus of Nazareth will destroy this place and change the customs which Moses delivered to us." Act 6:13-14

The English Revised Version translates the word "despisers" from kataphronetai as "scoffers" referring directly to the Jews in Antioch of Pisidia who rejected the gospel and mocked at the judgment coming upon them.

> Act 13:38-41 Let it be known to you therefore, brothers, that through this man forgiveness of sins is proclaimed to you, (39) and by him everyone who believes is freed from everything from which you could not be freed by the law of Moses. (40) Beware, therefore, lest what is said in the Prophets should come about: (41) "'Look, you scoffers, be astounded and perish; for I am doing a work in your days, a work that you will not believe, even if one tells it to you.'"

As we progress, we will demonstrate that Peter is teaching about the destruction of the temple, just as did Stephen. In other words, Peter's subject is the same as that in Matthew chapter 23:36-24:3, Lk. 21:20-22. This means that Peter would be in agreement of teaching a judgment that was about to destroy the city and temple of Jerusalem. For this reason, he encountered the scoffing Jews.

This is similar to what futurists do today when these verses of imminence are presented to them. They reject the words of inspiration and mock the teaching for a soon to occur event as an impossibility. They become scoffers! The presence of these modern day scoffers demonstrate and prove that there are those of us who teach that Christ's coming in the first century was imminent. Otherwise, why are they presently rejecting the full preterist view of an imminent first century coming of the Lord, if it were not being taught? In like manner, the scoffers would not have rejected and scoffed against Peter's message of imminence if the apostles had not taught that the coming was near in *their* lifetime!

Jude offers further evidence of the Judaic character of the scoffers. First, he says the apostles spoke of them, Jude 1:17. They were mockers (empaiktai). This is the precise same word used in 2 Peter 3:3 for the scoffers. Both Jude and Peter wrote about the same time. Paul writes specifically of the Judaizers who were persecuting Christians. The word he uses means to pursue and persecute. The Jews demonstrated this behavior in persecuting Paul in Thessalonica and in their pursuit of him to Berea to do the same. Paul refers to the story of Ishmael and Isaac. In Gen 21:9, the word used for Ishmael's mocking of Isaac is paidzo. It means the action of boys who rough up those smaller than they are. In each case, however, the Judaizers are intended. Further, Jude says they were sensual (natural, from psuchikos) persons, who cause divisions, not having the Spirit. Thus, a key mark of identification was their complete distinction from believers who had the Holy Spirit.

In the Galatians' epistle, when Paul spoke of those who did not have the Spirit, he said they were followers of the Torah, Gal 3:2-5.

(2) This only I want to learn from you: Did you receive the Spirit by the works of the law, or by the hearing of faith?—

(3) Are you so foolish? Having begun in the Spirit, are you now being made perfect by the flesh?

(4) Have you suffered so many things in vain—if indeed it was in vain?

(5) Therefore He who supplies the Spirit to you and works miracles among you, does He do it by the works of the law, or by the hearing of faith?

Therefore, those who did not have the Spirit were the Judaizers who chose Torah over the gospel of Christ. See also 1 Cor. 2:14-16. This also identifies the historical time frame of the Scoffers as the first century, pre-70AD. Why? It's because the activity of the Holy Spirit, i.e. the miracles were constrained to a period of 40 years paralleling that of the Exodus from Egypt. (Mal. 7:15, Acts 7:36, Heb. 3:7-10) Contextually, it is eisegesis to carry the activity of these scoffers beyond 70AD. This fact further demonstrates the imminence of the apostolic doctrine on the nearness of the end of all things.

Having identified the mockers as the Judaizers of the first century Peter rebuts their claim that all things were continuing from the time the father's (Abraham, Isaac and Jacob) fell asleep. Peter says that the Judaizers had willfully forgotten that *"by the word of God, the heavens were of old and the earth was standing out of the water and in the water, by which the world that then existed perished, being flooded with water." (3:5-6)*

In other words, Peter describes a world that existed prior to the fathers of Israel, i.e. (Abraham, Isaac and Jacob), that perished, namely in the flood of Noah. It was not the physical world that was destroyed, but according to the Genesis record, it was the "end of all flesh" (6:14). The flood waters were not the object of destruction, but rather, they were the agents of destruction. The flood waters were the means by which all flesh was destroyed. In both chapters 2 and 3, Peter makes this point.

> "and did not spare the ancient world, but saved Noah, one of eight people, a preacher of righteousness, bringing in the flood on the world of the ungodly;" 2Pe 2:5

> "For this they willfully forget: that by the word of God the heavens were of old, and the earth standing out of water and in the water, (6) by which the world that then existed perished, being flooded with water." (2Pe 3:5-6)

Note in each case, Peter says the flood water destroyed the "ungodly people". That was the "world" or "cosmos" that was destroyed by the flood, not the literal heavens and earth. Using this fact, he proceeds to show that the "heavens and earth" which then existed, would result in the destruction of "ungodly men." Those who claim that the text speaks of the literal destruction of the physical universe are referred to the texts discussed above where God promised never to destroy the physical creation.

Was there a world about to be destroyed at the time of 2 Peter's writings? Yes! Almost all the apostles speak of it, though in different ways. Note the messages of the Christ and the Apostles.

	1 Cor. 7:26, 10:11	Heb. 1:10,11 12:25, 26	1 John 2:17
"Tell us when will these things be? And what will be the sign of Your coming, and of the end of the age?"	The form of this world (cosmos) is passing away	You, Lord, in the beginning laid the foundation of the earth, and the heavens are the work of your hands. They will perish, but You remain; and they ill all grow old like a garment.	And the world (cosmos) is passing away, and the lust of it; but he who does the will of God abides forever.
Immediately after the tribulation of those days the sun will be darkened, and the moon will not give its light; the stars will fall from heaven, and the powers of the heavens will be shaken.	Now all these things happened to them as examples, and they were written for our admonition, upon whom the ends of the ages have come.	Whose voice then shook the earth but now He has promised, saying "Yet once more I shake not only the earth, but also heaven"	Then I saw a great white throne and Him who sat on it, from whose face the earth and the heaven fled away. And there was found no place for them.
Heaven and earth will pass away, but My words will by no means pass away.		Now this, "Yet once more, indications the removal of those things which are being shaken, that the things which cannot be shaken may remain.	Now I saw a new heaven and a new earth, for the first heaven and the first earth had passed away,. Also there was no more sea

Each of the texts show that the Lord and the Apostles taught that the heaven and earth, the world, and the age of their day was coming to an end.

Heaven and Earth

The heaven and earth spoken of in the text refers to Israel as a national kingdom and their temple. Josephus and Philo show how the temple represented heaven and earth:

> "As for the inside, Moses parted its length into three partitions. At the distance of ten cubits from the most secret end, Moses placed four pillars, the workmanship of which was the very same with that of the rest; and they stood upon the like bases with them, each a small matter distant from his fellow. Now the room within those pillars was the most holy place; but the rest of the room was the tabernacle, which was open for the priests. However, this proportion of the measures of the tabernacle proved to be an imitation of the system of the world; for that third part thereof which was within the four pillars, to which the priests were not admitted, is, as it were, a heaven peculiar to God. But the space of the twenty cubits, is, as it were, sea and land, on which men live, and so this part is peculiar to the priests only…"[20]

Priesthood Garments Modeled After The World

> "Now here one may wonder at the ill-will which men bear to us, and which they profess to bear on account of our despising that Deity which they pretend to honor; for if any one do but consider the fabric of the tabernacle, and take a view of the garments of the high priest, and of those vessels which we make use of in our sacred ministration, he will find that our legislator was a divine man, and that we are unjustly reproached by others; for if any one do without prejudice, and with judgment, look upon these things, he will find they were every one made in way of imitation and representation of the universe. When Moses distinguished the tabernacle into three parts, (15) and allowed two of them to the priests, as a place accessible and common, he denoted the land and the sea, these being of general access to all; but he set apart the third division for God, because heaven is inaccessible to men. And when he ordered twelve loaves to be set on the table, he denoted the year, as distinguished into so many months. By branching out the candlestick into seventy parts, he secretly intimated the Decani, or seventy divisions of the planets; and as to the

---

[20] Flavius Josephus, Antiquities of the Jews, Bk. 3.6.4

seven lamps upon the candlesticks, they referred to the course of the planets, of which that is the number. The veils, too, which were composed of four things, they declared the four elements; for the fine linen was proper to signify the earth, because the flax grows out of the earth; the purple signified the sea, because that color is dyed by the blood of a sea shell-fish; the blue is fit to signify the air; and the scarlet will naturally be an indication of fire. Now the vestment of the high priest being made of linen, signified the earth; the blue denoted the sky, being like lightning in its pomegranates, and in the noise of the bells resembling thunder. And for the ephod, it showed that God had made the universe of four elements; and as for the gold interwoven, I suppose it related to the splendor by which all things are enlightened. He also appointed the breastplate to be placed in the middle of the ephod, to resemble the earth, for that has the very middle place of the world. And the girdle which encompassed the high priest round, signified the ocean, for that goes round about and includes the universe. Each of the sardonyxes declares to us the sun and the moon; those, I mean, that were in the nature of buttons on the high priest's shoulders. And for the twelve stones, whether we understand by them the months, or whether we understand the like number of the signs of that circle which the Greeks call the Zodiac, we shall not be mistaken in their meaning. And for the mitre, which was of a blue color, it seems to me to mean heaven; for how otherwise could the name of God be inscribed upon it? That it was also illustrated with a crown, and that of gold also, is because of that splendor with which God is pleased. Let this explication (16) suffice at present, since the course of my narration will often, and on many occasions, afford me the opportunity of enlarging upon the virtue of our legislator."[21]

For there are, as it seems, two temples belonging to God; one being this world, in which the high priest is the divine word, his own firstborn son. The other is the rational soul, the priest of which is the real true man, the copy of whom, perceptible to the senses, is he who performs his paternal vows and sacrifices, to whom it is enjoined to put on the aforesaid tunic, the representation of the universal heaven, in order that the world may join with the man in offering sacrifice, and that the man may likewise co-operate with the universe.

He is now therefore shown to have these two things, the speckled and the variegated character. We will now proceed to explain the third and most perfect kind, which is denominated thoroughly white. When this same high priest enters into the innermost parts of the holy temple, he is clothed in the variegated garment, and he also assumes another linen robe, made of the very finest flax. (217) And this is an emblem of vigor, and incorruptibility, and the most brilliant light. For such a veil is a thing very difficult to be broken, and it is

---

[21] Ibid, 3:7.7

made of nothing mortal, and when it is properly and carefully purified it has a most clear and brilliant appearance. Philo On Dreams, Book I, 215-217, p. 384

(96) "For God intends that the high priest should in the first place have a visible representation of the universe about him, in order that from the continual sight of it he may be reminded to make his own life worthy of the nature of the universe, and secondly, in order that the whole world may co-operate with him in the performance of his sacred rites.

And it is exceedingly becoming that the man who is consecrated to the service of the Father of the world should also bring his son to the service of him who has begotten him.

(97) There is also a third symbol contained in this sacred dress, which it is important not to pass over in silence. For the priests of other deities are accustomed to offer up prayers and sacrifices solely for their own relations, and friends, and fellow citizens. But the high priest of the Jews offers them up not only on behalf of the whole race of mankind, but also on behalf of the different parts of nature, of the earth, of water, of air, and of fire; and pours forth his prayers and thanksgivings for them all, looking upon the world (as indeed it really is) as his country, for which, therefore, he is accustomed to implore and propitiate its governor by supplications and prayers, beseeching him to give a portion of his own merciful and humane nature to the things which he has created.[22]

These descriptions of the temple and priestly garments reflect the statements in the Bible that refer to the temple as heaven and earth. Moses addressed Israel as heaven and earth:

"Give ear, O heavens, and I will speak; And hear, O earth, the words of my mouth. Deu 32:1

Haggai spoke of the temple as "heaven and earth"

"For thus says the LORD of hosts: 'Once more (it is a little while) I will shake heaven and earth, the sea and dry land; (7) and I will shake all nations, and they shall come to the Desire of All Nations, and I will fill this temple with glory,' says the LORD of hosts. (8) 'The silver is Mine, and the gold is Mine,' says the LORD of hosts. (9) 'The glory of this latter temple shall be greater than the former,' says the LORD of hosts. 'And in this place I will give peace,' says the LORD of hosts." Hag. 2:6-9)

---

[22] Philo, XVII, p. 542

This text is quoted in Hebrews 12:26-27"

"whose voice then shook the earth; but now He has promised, saying, "YET ONCE MORE I SHAKE NOT ONLY THE EARTH, BUT ALSO HEAVEN." (27) Now this, "YET ONCE MORE," indicates the removal of those things that are being shaken, as of things that are made, that the things which cannot be shaken may remain."

Observe that not only is this a quote from Haggai, it also speaks of this heaven and earth being shaken so as to remove it. If this were the literal heaven, it would remove the universe requiring a complete replacement. Secondly, note that the phrase YET ONCE MORE is stated twice. This double mention is added for emphasis so that we pay the more careful attention to it. Thirdly, this heaven and earth was already "being shaken". It was already coming to its end. Lastly, the phrase, "as of things that are made" is an ellipsis for the phrase "made by hands". So the full meaning of the thought is "as of things that are made with hands". This is a contrast to the kingdom that remains mentioned in verse 28. The kingdom is "not made by hands". The first time the phrase "not made with hands" is used in the Bible is in Daniel chapter 2 where it speaks of the kingdom of God.

You watched while **a stone was cut out without hands**, which struck the image on its feet of iron and clay, and broke them in pieces. Dan 2:34

"And in the days of these kings the God of heaven will set up a kingdom which shall never be destroyed; and the kingdom shall not be left to other people; it shall break in pieces and consume all these kingdoms, and it shall stand forever. (45) Inasmuch as you saw that the stone was cut out of the mountain **without hands**, and that it broke in pieces the iron, the bronze, the clay, the silver, and the gold—the great God has made known to the king what will come to pass after this. The dream is certain, and its interpretation is sure." Dan 2:44-45 (emp. Mine, WB)

The stone cut out of the mountain without hands is the kingdom. It corresponds to the "house not made with hands" that Jesus promised to build, (Mk. 14:58). It is the dwelling place of God who said, "The Most High does not dwell in temples made with men's hands" (Isa.

66:1, Acts 7:48) It is in direct contrast to the temple built by Solomon in 1 Kings 8:27.

> "But will God indeed dwell on the earth? Behold, heaven and the heaven of heavens cannot contain You. How much less this temple which I have built!

The phrase made with hands reflects the words of Solomon who said, "How much less this temple which *I have built?* Thus, the temple made with men's hands is in direct contrast with the kingdom temple of God made without hands. This is why the kingdom is mentioned in direct contrast to the heaven and earth made by hands and was being shaken. The kingdom is the new heaven and earth not made with men's hands and is that which cannot be shaken per Heb. 12:28. In chapter 9 of Hebrews, the temple is also described as heaven and earth:

> "Then indeed, even the first covenant had ordinances of divine service and the earthly sanctuary. (2) For a tabernacle was prepared: the first part, in which was the lampstand, the table, and the showbread, which is called the sanctuary; (3) and behind the second veil, the part of the tabernacle which is called the Holiest of All," Heb 9:1-3

By divine service, the writer means the Most Holy Place where the high priest entered once a year to perform the *"heavenly services"*. The Holy place as described above represented the *earthly sanctuary* or the land. For all these reasons, the temple was the representation of the heaven and earth. So, when Peter spoke of the "heavens and earth" which are now, he spoke of the Old Covenant temple of God, that was in Jerusalem along with her people, most of whom were mocking and persecuting the church, and thus were marked for destruction. (See Matt. 23:37, 38, 24:3, 35, Lk. 21:20-22; Rev. 11:2). It was this arrangement that the Judaizers saw as continuing. However, Stephen, like Jesus before him had clearly spoke of its destruction, (Acts 6:12-14, Matt. 24:2f)

Since The Fathers Fell Asleep All Things Continue

Peter had taught that the end of *all things* had drawn near, 1 Pet. 4:7. The scoffers said, "since the fathers fell asleep, *all things* continue," more literally, *are continuing* as they were from [the] beginning of creation. The question naturally arises, which creation? Does he mean the Old

Covenant creation of Israel which began after the fathers, i.e. Abraham, Isaac and Jacob fell asleep? Or, does he mean the creation in Genesis 1-2? The next verse sheds light on the question.

> For this they willfully forget: that by the word of God the heavens were of old, and the earth standing out of water and in the water, (2Pe 3:5)

Peter's Counter Response to the Scoffers

Peter stated that the Judaizers were willfully ignorant of the fact that the heavens were of old and the earth was standing out of the water and in the water. What is meant by the heavens were of old? Some reason that this is the beginning of God's covenant with Adam as in "Covenant Creation". If that is true, why does Peter mention that the earth was standing out of the water and in the water in correlation to the heavens which were of old? Why contrast the heavens with the literal creation of water that partially covered the earth? Where is the concept of covenant creation? What role did covenant creation have in the flood waters that destroyed the Antedeluvian world? I admit that I could be totally blind in seeing covenant creation in the text, but flood waters do not appear on the surface to be metaphorical.

Jesus speaks of the flood in connection with the judgment of Noah saying the flood waters came and destroyed all the wicked. In like manner fire and brimstone rained from heaven to destroy the cities of Sodom and Gomorrah. And a "flood of fiery" of destruction would also come to destroy the temple and city of Jerusalem. Neither of these examples describes figurative or non-literal events. My conclusion is that the heavens which were of old with the earth standing in and out of water refer to the material creation and through that agency, the flood waters destroyed the people in the days of Noah.

The word "apo" means from or away from. It appears that the scoffers began their objection from the time that the father's fell asleep. Even if Adam were included in the fathers it would refer to a time after the creation of the physical world. However, as noted several times, I believe the fathers are Abraham, Isaac and Jacob. Therefore, from their days, the creation of Israel at Sinai continued up to the time of the scoffers. Peter had to redirect their thinking to the time before the fathers fell asleep, namely to the time of old when the heavens and earth were created. While it was before Israel's history, it showed the origins of the nation through Adam, Seth, Noah and Shem, and therefore was a valid record of their history which they had ignorantly and willfully overlooked. Peter's proof demonstrated that all things had not continued because there was a flood that interrupted the flow of the world in a destruction which came upon the world of the ungodly. He had already mentioned this once in chapter two right along with the destruction that occurred in the days of Lot, both of which should have been a warning to them. These events were cited to corroborate the judgment Peter mentioned in the first three verses that for a long time were laid up for their generation.

> (1) But there were also false prophets among the people, even as there will be false teachers among you, who will secretly bring in destructive heresies, even denying the Lord who bought them, and bring on themselves swift destruction. (2) And many will follow their destructive ways, because of whom the way of truth will be blasphemed. (3) By covetousness they will exploit you with deceptive words; for a long time their judgment has not been idle, and their destruction does not slumber. (2Pe 2:1-3)

Peter spoke of the false teachers among the people during the time of the O.T. prophets to remind his first century audience that they too would experience the false prophets. In addition, they would deny the Lord who bought them and bring upon themselves, "swift destruction". Swift is from "tachos" and means "swift, quick and impending". In other words it was a judgment that was already hanging over their heads and about to come. The persuasiveness of these false teachers would persuade the very believers Peter addressed. However, their judgment that was appointed for them of a long time ago did not sleep, indicating it was ready to occur. He then cites three major judgments that had occurred as proof that God would judge the wicked of his day.

This is why Peter said the heavens and the earth which are now (meaning now in his day) were reserved for fire until the day of judgment and perdition of ungodly men. The words Peter uses here are very significant. They point to the Old Testament source from which Peter draws his language for a fiery destruction upon the nation of the Jews of his day. First, we have the word preserved from τεθησαυρισμένοι, (tethēsaurismenoi). This is the word from which our word "thesaurus" is derived. It means to store up, treasure up, to save, lay up, , to amass or reserve. This is a judgment that was stored up or saved by God for the proper time. This word is found in Moses' farewell speech to Israel before his death, in the Song of Moses, where he speaks of Israel's end.

> (34) "Is this not laid up in store with Me, Sealed up among My treasures?" (35) Vengeance is Mine, and recompense; Their foot shall slip in due time; For the day of their calamity is at hand, And the things to come hasten upon them.' (36) "For the LORD will judge His people And have compassion on His servants, When He sees that their power is gone, And there is no one remaining, bond or free. Deu 32:34-36

The Hebrew equivalent of thesauros is *kamus*, and means laid up in store. The LXX (Septuagint) translates it as, θησαυροις (thesauros), a deposit, that is wealth, a treasure, hence the idea of storing or saving it up for the proper time and use. Note that the verse speaks of the time of God's vengeance when he would judge his people saying that the day of their calamity would be "at hand" or near. This is the judgment which had been laid up or stored up for a long time that Peter said was about to come in his day and upon the Judaizers of his generation.

Secondly, the words "laid up in store among my treasures" are from the Hebrew, *beowsrotay* (my treasures) and *hatum* (sealed up) which means to stamp (with a signet or private mark) for security or preservation (literally or figuratively); by implication to keep secret). This means the judgment time was only known by God and answers to Zech. 14:6, the day known only to the Lord, and Matthew 24:36, the day which no man knew but the Father until it was revealed. Peter is therefore quoting from this very source to teach about God's judgment that had been sealed or treasured up for Israel since the time of Moses. The reader is encouraged to become very familiar with the entire Song of Moses in Deuteronomy 32.

Thirdly, it is also from this chapter that Peter quotes the language of a "fiery" destruction.

(21) They have provoked Me to jealousy by what is not God; They have moved Me to anger by their foolish idols. But I will provoke them to jealousy by those who are not a nation; I will move them to anger by a foolish nation. (22) For a fire is kindled in My anger, And shall burn to the lowest hell; It shall consume the earth with her increase, And set on fire the foundations of the mountains. (Deu 32:21-22)

Israel provoked God to jealousy by following idols, forsaking her marriage covenant and thus moved him to anger. Thus, in their last days God would provoke them to anger by those who were not a nation, (Rom 10:19, 11:11, 12). Because of Israel's provocation, a "fire was kindled in Yahweh's anger" that would burn to the lowest gehenna. It would consume the earth with her increase (destroy all of Israel's crops causing famine and pestilence" and set on fire the foundations of the mountains. The metaphor of setting the mountains on fire demonstrates God's presence in judgment. We can look back to Exodus 19, and see where at God's presence the mountains burned and quaked with fire. The symbolism derives from this event and others like the burning bush to represent God's Presence. It is also used in Micah to describe the judgment on the day of the Lord:

(2) Hear, all you peoples! Listen, O earth, and all that is in it! Let the Lord GOD be a witness against you, The Lord from His holy temple.

(3) For behold, the LORD is coming out of His place; He will come down And tread on the high places of the earth.

(4) The mountains will melt under Him, And the valleys will split Like wax before the fire, Like waters poured down a steep place.

(5) All this is for the transgression of Jacob And for the sins of the house of Israel. What is the transgression of Jacob? Is it not Samaria? And what are the high places of Judah? Are they not Jerusalem?

(6) "Therefore I will make Samaria a heap of ruins in the field, Places for planting a vineyard; I will pour down her stones into the valley, And I will uncover her foundations. (Mic 1:2-6)

Note at God's Presence or coming out of His place (the temple), he comes down out of "heaven" to tread on the earth. The mountains melt under his feet because he is a consuming fire. Yahweh does not have literal feet, nor is this literal fire that melts literal mountains. It is, however, the destruction during the reigns of Jotham, Ahaz and Hezekiah concerning

Samaria and Jerusalem c. 740 B.C. to about 680 B.C.[23] This is apocalyptic or metaphoric language used to describe the judgment upon Israel by the Assyrians. The statement that the valley would split is similar to the language used in Zechariah 14:5, where the Mt. of Olives would split, during the time of the destruction of Jerusalem in 70AD. Again, the language is not to be taken literally. The same prophetic apocalyptic metaphor is used in Isaiah 34 to speak of the fall of Edom.

> [1] Come near, you nations, to hear; And heed, you people! Let the earth hear, and all that is in it, The world and all things that come forth from it.
>
> [2] For the indignation of the LORD is against all nations, And His fury against all their armies; He has utterly destroyed them, He has given them over to the slaughter.
>
> [3] Also their slain shall be thrown out; Their stench shall rise from their corpses, And the mountains shall be melted with their blood. (Isa 34:1-3)

Compare this reading with that in Micah and note the striking similarities. It is in this genre of language that the prophets spoke of fire as a symbol of destruction by a foreign nation employed by God as his servant to punish Israel and in some cases other nations for their sins.

A Day Is as A Thousand Years and A Thousand Years as One Day

This is perhaps one of the most abused texts in all of Scripture. Over-zealous but ill-informed interpreters misuse it to teach the very opposite of what Peter taught. In fact, they use it thinking they are supporting Peter when they are actually contradicting him and making the SCOFFERS ARGUMENT!!! We have shown that Peter taught that the coming salvation, and coming of the Lord was imminent from 1 Peter 1:6-8, namely that it was ready or prepared and coming after they suffered a little while. Hebrews 10:37 supports this saying that the Christ would come in a very, very little while without delay. In chapter 4:5, he said God was ready to judge the living and the dead, 4:5 that the end of all things had drawn near, 4:7 and that the time for the judgment

---

[23] NICNT, e-Sword Version

to begin at the house of God had come, 4:17. In chapter 5:1, he taught that the glory was about to be revealed at Christ's coming. As stated above, he said that the 2 Peter 3 was a reminder of the teaching in the first epistle, along with that of the Lord and the apostles. Therefore, everything Peter, the Christ and the apostles taught about the coming of the Lord is that it was near, soon to come, at hand and imminent. But the scoffers asked where was that promise. They claimed it was not near. They were saying it would not occur. Now ask yourself, would Peter use a text to **agree** with the Scoffers or would he further develop the argument and teaching he already established. Does anyone debate by making the opponents argument to prove their point when the opponent teaches something radically different than what they are teaching? Would a futurist who believes that Christ's coming was a literal thousand years or more use the language of verse 8, to teach that it meant a coming in the first century? Absolutely not! Rather, they use it to claim the coming was at least a thousand years in the future and could not possibly have been at hand.

However, if they were teaching as Peter taught that the coming was near, would they contradict themselves by using a verse that taught that coming was centuries off into the future? Do we actually believe the Holy Spirit or the Apostle Peter was that ignorant and uninformed? What is the point? Peter uses the statement in verse 8 to further buttress the arguments he's already made in saying that the coming judgment was soon to occur. This is how the statement is used in its original context and in the manner in which Peter uses it. He does not, as the futurists are fond of doing, making the scoffers argument who said the coming was not at hand. Let us examine the verse.

> But, beloved, do not forget this one thing, that with the Lord one day is as a thousand years, and a thousand years as one day. (2Pe 3:8)

The original source of this text is found in Psalms 90, a Psalm of Moses. The entire psalm is listed here for your observation and convenience. A Prayer Of Moses the Man of God.

> (1) LORD, You have been our dwelling place in all generations.

(2) Before the mountains were brought forth, Or ever You had formed the earth and the world, Even from everlasting to everlasting, You are God.

(3) You turn man to destruction, And say, "Return, O children of men."

(4) For a thousand years in Your sight Are like yesterday when it is past, And like a watch in the night.

(5) You carry them away like a flood; They are like a sleep. In the morning they are like grass which grows up:

(6) In the morning it flourishes and grows up; In the evening it is cut down and withers.

(7) For we have been consumed by Your anger, And by Your wrath we are terrified.

(8) You have set our iniquities before You, Our secret sins in the light of Your countenance.

(9) For all our days have passed away in Your wrath; We finish our years like a sigh.

(10) The days of our lives are seventy years; And if by reason of strength they are eighty years, Yet their boast is only labor and sorrow; For it is soon cut off, and we fly away.

(11) Who knows the power of Your anger? For as the fear of You, so is Your wrath.

(12) So teach us to number our days, That we may gain a heart of wisdom.

(13) Return, O LORD! How long? And have compassion on Your servants.

(14) Oh, satisfy us early with Your mercy, That we may rejoice and be glad all our days!

(15) Make us glad according to the days in which You have afflicted us, The years in which we have seen evil.

(16) Let Your work appear to Your servants, And Your glory to their children.

(17) And let the beauty of the LORD our God be upon us, And establish the work of our hands for us; Yes, establish the work of our hands. (Psa 90:1-17)

As shown above, this is a Psalm of Moses. It speaks of the ever-lasting God, and then quickly moves to a discussion of God turning man to destruction and of his need to repent. Notice that the verse following verse 8 (2 Peter 3:9), is also a call to repentance. So we have a similar theme in Psalm 90 as that found in 2 Peter 3:9. The reason they are called to repent is *"For a thousand years in Your sight Are like yesterday when it is past and like a watch in the night"*. Moses gave two illustrations along with the mention of the thousand years. He said it was "like yesterday when it is past". How long is a day? Is it not but 24 hours. It comes quickly and goes quickly. The older we get, seemly the faster the days pass us by. Next, he said a thousand years were like a "watch in the night." This shows us that Moses is using the term to describe very short and swiftly passing events. For the Jews, the night was divided into three watches of four hours each. Thus, a single watch was only four hours, another very short period of time. The Romans divided the night into four watches of only three hours each, an even shorter period? Why is Moses comparing the thousand years to these very short periods of time if it were meant to teach a millennium or literal thousand years? How does that compare with a 4 hour watch in the night?

Next, he uses being carried away like a flood. The waters of a flood move very swiftly, sweeping away everything in its path. I watched a video of a fitness trainer who jumped from a cliff into a sea with waves violently dashing against the rocks. Seeing her in danger, her friend, also a health fitness coach tried to help her. Apparently, they considered themselves strong swimmers. However, in a matter of minutes, the waves resisted their efforts of rescue to safety and swept them out to sea in less than a minute, all captured on video. This was not a flood, but raging waves splashing against rocks. The momentum of a flood, i.e. one that lifts and floats houses from their foundations, sweeps away tall buildings and trees, not to mention cars and people, move dangerously fast. This is what the thousand years is compared to in the text. Remember, this text is the source of 2 Peter 3:8.

Then Moses says the thousand years are like a sleep. At the most, that's about 8 hours for many people but even less for the insomniacs. It passes quickly. In verse 6, he compares it to grass which comes up in the morning, and is mowed down in the evening so that it withers. Again we must ask, why is every illustration of the thousand years used by Moses referring to something that passes quickly versus a thousand years or more?

Then Moses moves back to the real theme of the Psalm. It is about Yahweh's wrath upon Israel. "For we have been consumed by Your anger, and by Your wrath we are terrified, (v. 7). Of what anger and wrath does Moses speak? We must appeal to the Exodus narrative. When Israel received the Torah by Moses, they made a golden calf and turned back in their hearts to worship the idols of Egypt. God's wrath was kindled against them. When Israel sinned God told Moses to get down from the mountain because they had corrupted themselves in making, worshiping and offering sacrifices to a molded calf. They also claimed it was the god that led them out of Egypt. The next words demonstrate the anger and wrath of God against them.

> (9) And the LORD said to Moses, "I have seen this people, and indeed it is a stiff-necked people!
>
> (10) Now therefore, let Me alone, that My wrath may burn hot against them and I may consume them. And I will make of you a great nation."
>
> (11) Then Moses pleaded with the LORD his God, and said: "LORD, why does Your wrath burn hot against Your people whom You have brought out of the land of Egypt with great power and with a mighty hand?
>
> (12) Why should the Egyptians speak, and say, 'He brought them out to harm them, to kill them in the mountains, and to consume them from the face of the earth'? Turn from Your fierce wrath, and relent from this harm to Your people. (Exo 32:9-12)

Notice verses 10, 11, and 12, refer to God's wrath. This is the wrath that Moses refers to in the Psalm. So we ask the question, how long did God's wrath against Israel continue? Hebrews 3:7-9, says he was angry with that generation for forty years. So the thousand years is found in the context of the Exodus, a period of about 40 years. That is about the same time of God's wrath upon the Jews for crucifying Christ and persecuting the saints. Is it merely a coincidence that Peter selects a verse from this Psalm to speak of God's wrath on Jews by the Roman invasion and destruction of the Jerusalem and the temple?

The Longsuffering of God

God's longsuffering refers to the time he gave Israel to repent for the crucifixion of Christ and the persecution and martyrs of the saints. He was long-suffering because he didn't want anyone from Israel to perish but to come to repentance. However, they despised His goodness and treasured up for themselves wrath against the day of wrath. See Romans 2:3-5.

The Day of the Lord

The Day of the Lord is the term used for God's judgment upon Israel and in other cases upon the nations. It is very a very common expression in the Prophets. When Israel or another nation sinned and filled their cup of iniquity God would judge them? This was called the day of the Lord. The main point here is to understand that the phrase "day of the Lord" is not used to point to some catastrophic destruction of the physical world. We have shown this to be a false concept and is not based on Scripture. Yet, traditions are strongly implanted in the minds of the masses, and even those who claim to be teachers of truth.

Joel speaks of the "day of the Lord" in the following verses, 1:15, 2:1, 11, 31 and 3:14. Amos speaks of it as the "day of the Lord," (5:18, 20) and the "day of doom", (6:3) See also Zephaniah 1:7, 14-16. Zechariah uses the phrase that day or "in that day, 12:4, 6, 8, 9, 11, 13:1, 2, 4; 14:1, 6, 8, 9, 13, 21. In Malachi it is the "day of His coming" and the "day which is coming" (3:2, 4:1) and the "great and dreadful day," 4:5. Obadiah uses the phrases "day of their calamity," 1:13, "day of distress," 1:14 and "day of the Lord," 1:15. Some describe the destruction of Jerusalem, first by the Chaldeans and lastly by the Roman invasion of Judea. Others speak of the fall of pagan nations such as Edom, Nineveh. Each must be determined by the context. Some occurrences merely speak of "the day," or some other description of the day of the Lord such as "day of darkness, or day of thick clouds, Joel 2:2, or simply as the day, (Heb. 10:25). The New Testament draws from this language in the prophets referring to it as "that day", (Matthew 24:36) "the great and terrible day of the Lord' Acts 2:20, "the day of wrath", (Rom. 2:5) "the day" (Heb. 10:25), "the day of the Lord, 2 Pet. 3:10, the "day of God" (2 Pet. 3:12) "the day of judgment," (1 John 4:17), and "the Lord's day." In the New Testament they all point to the one and same day of the Lord, i.e. the destruction of Jerusalem and the temple in 70AD.

As A Thief in the Night

Peter writes that the day of the Lord would come as a thief in the night. He again is quoting from the Prophets. Joel, speaking of the invading army said, "They enter the windows like a thief", (Joel 2:9). This was the manner in which the Chaldeans invaded Jerusalem. In all of God's judgments upon the wicked, he came like a thief in the day. Concerning the flood, Luke writes "they knew not until the flood came and took them all away". He says the same of Lot concerning Sodom and Gomorrah. They carried on the normal affairs of life until the day God rained fire and brimstone from heaven. (Luke 17:26-28) Likewise, the judgment upon Egypt came unawares upon the whole house of Pharaoh. The terror struck them at midnight, Ex. 12:29-31. The destruction of Jerusalem by the Babylonians in 586 B.C. occurred at night when they were observing the Passover, totally unexpected. Yet, none of these judgments related to the end of the physical world. They all occurred in time, though the victims were taken by surprise.

In like manner, Peter speaks of the judgment upon Jerusalem in 66-70AD as taking them unawares as a thief in the night. Just like the Chaldeans, the Romans invaded Jerusalem at the time of the Passover, which would have been at night, and totally unsuspected. Yet, the believers (Christians) were well informed and had already departed from the city, Matt. 24:15-18. So the phrase "the Lord would come as a thief in the night" does not mean that everyone was in the dark. Only the wicked and impenitent ones who refused to obey the Lord were in the dark. This is what Paul tells the Thessalonians.

> But concerning the times and the seasons, brethren, you have no need that I should write to you. (2) For you yourselves know perfectly that the day of the Lord so comes as a thief in the night. (3) For when they say, "Peace and safety!" then sudden destruction comes upon them, as labor pains upon a pregnant woman. And they shall not escape. (4) But you, brethren, are not in darkness, so that this Day should overtake you as a thief. (5) You are all sons of light and sons of the day. We are not of the night nor of darkness. 1Th 5:1-5

Notice that Paul said there was no need to write the Thessalonians about the time of the day of the Lord because it would come as a thief in the night. He said when "they" say? Of whom does he speak? He speaks of the enemies of the Lord who would not have him to reign over them. He is speaking of the Jews, those who killed the Lord Jesus, and persecuted the apostles and saints, 1 Thes. 2:14. He said the wrath would come upon them to the uttermost. When they felt safe and secure behind the gates of the city, that is when sudden destruction came upon them. Sudden is from "aiphnidios" and means to catch unawares, off guard, hence Paul says it was "as labor pains upon a pregnant woman". No one knew the day and hour of her labor pains, but only the foolish would not recognize that she was pregnant. Such was the negligence and arrogance of the unbelieving Jews to the Lord's warnings and pleas for their repentance which they ignored. They could not escape because the Romans had surrounded them, and built embankments all around the city so they could not escape. However, the believers were not in darkness that the day would overtake them as a thief. They departed from the city as the Lord warned them and escaped. The light of God's word, and their obedience kept them from being overtaken as a thief.

John, in Revelation, uses the same analogy and meaning, of "coming as a thief". Note carefully the words he recorded of Christ to the church in Sardis. He tells them to remember how they had been forewarned, and thus were to hold fast and watch and repent. A humble spirit will obey the Lord. Only if they did not take heed to the Lord's words, would they be taken unawares.

> Remember therefore how you have received and heard; hold fast and repent. Therefore if you will not watch, I will come upon you as a thief, and you will not know what hour I will come upon you. Rev 3:3

Compare also Revelation 16:15. The one who watched and kept his garments would not be found naked.

> "Behold, I am coming as a thief. Blessed is he who watches, and keeps his garments, lest he walk naked and they see his shame." Rev 16:15

Noah, Lot, and the faithful in Israel were never in darkness. They heeded the signs given and were spared of judgment. Only the wicked were overtaken as a thief. This is the meaning of Jesus' words in Matt.

24:42-43. It is the watching faithfulness that prevents being overtaken as a thief.

Therefore, Peter's words warn the scoffers and any who would follow their teaching that they would be overcome, hence the need to repent and watch.

Elements Melt with Fervent Heat

The elements are perhaps the second most misunderstood word in Peter's discussion of the end times. Almost immediately, those who opt for an "end of the physical world" interpretation, read this word at face value without doing any further study. They assume that Peter, who along with John were formally uneducated men, referred to as "ignorant and unlearned" would have had knowledge of the scientific periodic table. Thus, they reason, that he is speaking of Hydrogen, Oxygen, Lithium, and Nitrogen, etc. There is nothing in the context of 2 Peter that suggests a reference to the periodic table. The chemical table of elements was unknown before the 1700's at least as we know it today. That is long after Peter lived. So what does the word elements mean? Since we are attempting to understand the scriptures, why not allow the scriptures to interpret it? Isn't that the best approach?

The word translated elements is from the Greek word, stocheion. Thayer offers the following meanings:

[1] any first thing, from which the others belonging to some series or composite whole take their rise, an element, first principal

[1a] the letters of the alphabet as the elements of speech, not however the written characters, but the spoken sounds

[1b] the elements from which all things have come, the material causes of the universe

[1c] the heavenly bodies, either as parts of the heavens or (as others think) because in them the elements of man, life and destiny were supposed to reside

[1d] the elements, rudiments, primary and fundamental principles of any art, science, or discipline

[1d1] i.e. of mathematics, Euclid's geometry

In all the definitions given by Thayer, only one focuses on the universe. However, the rest consistently focus on the first or rudiments of a series, or system. Let us examine the a few texts to see which of the definitions fit.

> (3) Even so we, when we were children, were in bondage under the elements of the world. (4) But when the fullness of the time had come, God sent forth His Son, born of a woman, born under the law, (5) to redeem those who were under the law, that we might receive the adoption as sons. Gal 4:3-5

Paul says that the Jews were in bondage under the elements (stocheia) of the world. But, that they were delivered or redeemed from the law, in order to become the sons of God. Was Paul and the believing Jews delivered from the physical world? Did they no longer use water for drinking and fire to warm them and cook their food? Was anyone today who was redeemed by Christ redeemed from the physical world? If the stoicheion (elements) refer to the physical universe, then it means that the only way to escape them is to be redeemed by Christ. Otherwise, one would be stuck in the physical world forever, world without end! How reasonable is that? It is obvious that when Paul uses "elements of the world" he is not speaking of the physical world. He speaks of being under the law. It is from the law that they were redeemed, and that is how they receive the adoption to become sons of God. Compare Romans 8:14-15 where the subject is the same.

> For as many as are led by the Spirit of God, these are sons of God. (15) For you did not receive the spirit of bondage again to fear, but you received the Spirit of adoption by whom we cry out, "Abba, Father." Rom 8:14-15

The Spirit of bondage refers to the "yoke of the law" Israel received while in Sinai (Exodus 19). This is contrasted with the freedom from bondage received through the gospel. Paul wrote, stand fast in the liberty where Christ has made us free and do not be entangled again in a yoke of bondage, Gal. 5:1.

Paul refers to the weak and beggarly elements.

> But now after you have known God, or rather are known by God, how is it that you turn again to the weak and beggarly elements, to which you desire again to be in bondage? Gal 4:9

This text proves that it was through conversion that the saints were freed from the elements of the world. However, by going back to the law, they were returning to the bondage from which they had been redeemed. Can a person who was delivered from the physical world return to it by apostatizing after death? It is impossible. So, the "elements of the world" will not work in these passages.

If the elements of the world are the rudiments from which the universe was made, how could they be called weak and beggarly? We learned above that the physical universe would never be destroyed, and that it would continue long as the name of Yahweh. If it is weak and beggarly, what does that say of Yahweh's name? But, the scriptures do speak of the weakness of the law referring to its inability to save man from sins because of man's weakness.

> (18) For on the one hand there is an annulling of the former commandment because of its weakness and unprofitableness, (19) for the law made nothing perfect; on the other hand, there is the bringing in of a better hope, through which we draw near to God. Heb 7:18-19

The same meaning applies in Colossians 2:8, 20.

> Beware lest anyone cheat you through philosophy and empty deceit, according to the tradition of men, according to the basic principles of the world, and not according to Christ. Col 2:8

It is generally assumed that Paul is addressing Gnostics in Colossians. This is incorrect. He addresses those with a knowledge of the Exodus themes, using such terms as inheritance, kingdom, redemption, His blood [Passover] and forgiveness which would be associated with atonement, Rom. 1:12-14. Other terms associated with the Exodus motif are "firstborn", v. 18. He reiterates the Passover theme, in v 20, and speaks about "reconciliation (for iniquity)" a term used in Daniel 9:24. Again, verse 23, refers to atonement, where one may stand without reproach in Yahweh's temple presence in the Holy of holies. Other terms related to Israel are "circumcision", the handwriting of ordinances, Sabbaths new moons and festivals, (2:11-16) and heavenly things in Christ versus the land, (3:1-2).

Earth and all the Works Burned Up.

These terms are focused on Israel and the old covenant versus the gospel. Paul, therefore, warns the church to not be spoiled according to the traditions of men. Compare Matt. 15:3, 8, 9. Thus, the philosophy and vain deceit was that of the Judaizers and their attempt to turn the believers away from the faith, back to the weak and beggarly elements (stoicheia) of the law. That is the meaning of the basic "stoicheia" of the world (kosmos) which was not according to Christ or the gospel, Col. 2:8. This is further strengthened from verse 20:

> Therefore, if you died with Christ from the basic principles of the world, why, as though living in the world, do you subject yourselves to regulations— Col 2:20

Again, how could Paul write to people who had died to the physical elements of the world? Would that not be an absurd interpretation for this text? Yes, they died, but when and how? They were buried with Christ by baptism into death, releasing them from their sins and the law, Col. 2:11-12. It is the same as in Galatians 4:3. They were not released from the physical world, nor had they died to it. These verses show a consistency in the use of the "elements" of the world to refer to the bondage under sin and the law.

Paul again writes to Hebrews, this time to those who lived in the heart of Jerusalem, where those most zealous for the law resided. They are being scattered from the city and are being urged not to return to it, 13:10-14. In chapter five, he admonishes them about the first principles, saying they had not yet learned the basics. The law pointed them to Christ. It was their tutor to bring them to Christ. By going back to it, some had failed to learn that basic meaning of the law.

> For though by this time you ought to be teachers, you need someone to teach you again the first principles of the oracles of God; and you have come to need milk and not solid food. Heb 5:12

The Hebrews being the most exposed to the best teachers of the law, should have learned its basic tenets. However, because their conduct in turning back to it demonstrated their lack of learning, Paul said they needed to relearn or be taught again the basic elements (stoichea) of the oracles of God. By oracles, he means the law. (Rom. 3:2) Chapter six does not use the term stocheion, but the word is implied. The translators inserted the word principles because it made sense. The writer yet urges the audience to leave the first principles in order that they may go on to perfection. The language is even more emphatic. The word aphentes is used and it means having left the first principles (teachings of Moses) they were to complete their pilgrimage by going on to perfection or to the heavenly things in Christ, (Heb. 12:18-23. The terms, repentance from dead works, faith toward God, doctrines of baptisms, laying on of hands, etc, all represent the Torah an its altars and judgments.

With this knowledge, we return to 2 Peter 3:10. We have seen the consistent use of stoicheion, i.e. the elements as a reference to the basic and rudimentary principles of the law. Is Peter changing the meaning of the term to describe a different scenario? Everything we have shown in both epistles referred to the imminent end of the temple understood by them to be the heaven and earth, and it's wicked people in that first century generation.

What is the meaning of the great noise? Beginning with the fall of Jericho, God always used the noise of trumpets to accompany destruction. See Joshua 6:4f. Loud trumpets and noise were also association with the coming of God's presence as in Mt. Sinai, when the Lord visited Israel, Ex. 19:16, 19. Now, the two ideas are combined for we have both the coming of the Lord's presence and the destruction of the city, hence the symbolism of the "loud noise". This text is also parallel to Matt. 24:31, 1 Cor. 15:51, and 1 Thes. 4:16, all of which mention the sound of the trumpet used to gather together the elect from the four winds. However, in 2 Thessalonians 2:1, the saints were already being gathered to the Lord in view of his coming yet there were no literal trumpets sounding. Again, these are figures of apocalyptic or metaphoric language used to describe these events. The prophets recorded the same imagery to describe the day of the Lord in their day and time. See Joel 2:1, 5, Nahum 1:14, 16. Further, the chariots wheels would sound like the approach of thunder as they rolled along the fields stirring up dust clouds along the way.

The Elements Melt with Fervent Heat

Once again, this is the apocalyptic use of these terms to describe the end of the temple and city. Further, the temple veil had four literal elements woven into its construction, namely, earth, air, fire, and water. So, in one sense, the destruction of the temple was also the destruction of these elements. The temple was literally burned to the ground, and the gold and silver literally melted off the doors and walls. Since the destruction of the temple meant the end of the Levitical priesthood, that also meant the end of the Old Covenant.

The Works Burned

The works are the "works of the Law". These included the duties of the priests and Levites performed in the temple and the efforts of the people in trying to obtain justification through the law. All were brought to an end.

All These Things Are Being Dissolved

For some reason, perhaps due to the influence of futurism, the translators translated the *lyomenon* as "will be dissolved". However, the verb is a present middle or passive participle. Roy Runyon pointed out in one of his studies on 2 Peter that the correct translation of this word is "being dissolved". That is extremely important. What it demonstrates is that the world and elements Peter described were already being destroyed. That means it is a parallel to the temple we discussed above in Hebrews 12:26 which says "Now this, 'Yet once more,' indicates the removal of those things that are *being shaken*, as of things that are made [with men's hands], a clear reference to the temple. In other words, the judgment had begun. The shaking and dissolving of that temple cultus was already underway. Thus, Peter does not describe a destruction thousands of years in the future, but a judgment already underway in his time. Thus, the scoffers were doubly wrong, in asking where is the promise of His coming? All they had to do was pay attention to what was happening around them and they would have seen that the signs clearly showed the destruction was underway. It is for this reason, Peter urged his readers to be on point in their holy conduct and godliness. Otherwise, it would have been a warning for future generations as Moses admonished them in his "Song of Moses", Deut. 32.

Looking for and Hastening the Coming of the Day of God

This verse points us back to Deuteronomy 32 and the Song of Moses. The word "hasten" is a direct quote. Hasten in Hebrew is the word "koosh" and means to hurry. In the LXX it is translated as hetoima, the same word Peter used twice in the first epistle to speak of the time as ready for the fulfillment of the salvation at the revelation of Christ. The saints were looking with eagerness for this day to come in their generation. We have commented on the elements melting with fervent heat and refer the reader to our remarks above.

We Look for New Heavens and A New Earth

It follows that if the Old Heaven and Earth were the old covenant Temple and its people, then the New Heavens and earth must be the new covenant Temple and its people. That is precisely what the promise of the new heavens and earth says in Isaiah 65.

(17) "For behold, I create new heavens and a new earth; And the former shall not be remembered or come to mind.

(18) But be glad and rejoice forever in what I create; For behold, I create Jerusalem as a rejoicing, And her people a joy.

(19) I will rejoice in Jerusalem, And joy in My people; The voice of weeping shall no longer be heard in her, Nor the voice of crying." Isa 65:17-19

The former things of which the Prophet speaks are those related to the Old Covenant world. Once the new covenant arrived, they would no longer be remembered as a valid covenant before God or His new people. Observe that the new heavens and new earth is a newly created Jerusalem. Only this time, she is created a rejoicing, and her people are a joy. The rejoicing stands over against the mourning experienced from the bondage of living under the Old Covenant world. It is demonstrated with Israel under the bondage of Pharaoh in Egypt. Many who read about the weeping and crying erroneously assume that the conditions of the natural world with its wars, crimes, hurts and pains are what is meant in the text. This is incorrect. These are tears related to living under the powers of the bondage of captivity to sin and the reign of death that created fear and terror in the lives of the old covenant people. The story of the Exodus and Babylonian captivities provide for us a clear picture.

Crying and Groaning in Egypt

When Israel was in bondage in Egypt, they were afflicted by Pharaoh and his taskmasters. They were made to serve rigorously and were given very little resources to work with and to sustain themselves. In time these burdens became very great and they began to cry out to Yahweh because of these burdens.

> Now it happened in the process of time that the king of Egypt died. Then the children of Israel groaned because of the bondage, and they cried out; and their cry came up to God because of the bondage. (24) So God heard their groaning, and God remembered His covenant with Abraham, with Isaac, and with Jacob. (25) And God looked upon the children of Israel, and God acknowledged them. Exo 2:23-25

It is important to note that Israel groaned not because there were murders, violence, stomach pains, toothaches or hemorrhoids, etc. Rather, their groaning was specific. They groaned because of the bondage and they cried out because of it. God did not spend His time trying to dry the tears from every weeping eye in Israel. He heard babies crying, mother's crying over the loss of their children or husbands, men crying over inured limbs or other maladies. Just as today, Yahweh leaves us to use our own resources for comfort, i.e. medicine, doctors, counselors, etc. to remedy those things. The groaning here got Yahweh's attention. One reason it did, is because of the time. Does anyone believe that Israel groaned only after the Pharaoh who oppressed them died? That would be absurd. Would anyone say there were no crocodile tears in Israel until this occurred? There is a reason God heard Israel's groaning and cries at this specific moment in history. When we look in verse 24, we find the answer. God heard Israel's groans at this specific moment in history because they reminded Him of the covenant he made with Abraham, Isaac and Jacob. This was the time that the promise had drawn near for Israel to be delivered from bondage as God promised Abraham in Gen. 15:13-18. This was the fourth generation from the time the promise was given. Therefore, the time had come for Israel to be delivered from Egyptian bondage. Thus, their crying and groaning related to bondage would soon come to an end, but not until Israel journeyed through the wilderness. They continued groaning even through the wilderness because at this time, their minds had been subjected to the psychological effects of slavery and Egyptian culture. It was not until they reached the Promised land that the reproach of Egypt was rolled away.

(7) Then Joshua circumcised their sons whom He raised up in their place; for they were uncircumcised, because they had not been circumcised on the way. (8) So it was, when they had finished circumcising all the people, that they stayed in their places in the camp till they were healed. (9) Then the LORD said to Joshua, "This day I have rolled away the reproach of Egypt from you." Therefore the name of the place is called Gilgal to this day. Jos 5:7-9

So, it was a total of 40 years before Israel's groaning and crying from the bondage of Egypt ceased. Once they entered the land of Canaan, there was no more crying because of the bondage of Egypt. Yahweh dried their tears by redeeming them out of Egypt and bringing them into the new land of promise. This is the basis and meaning behind no more crying and tears.

Babylonian Captivity

A second example of crying over bondage results from the Babylonian captivity. When the southern kingdom of Judah was carried captive, they wept in Babylon because of their bondage. The 137th Psalm captures the sentiments of this captivity.

(1) By the rivers of Babylon, There we sat down, yea, we wept When we remembered Zion. (2) We hung our harps Upon the willows in the midst of it.

(3) For there those who carried us away captive asked of us a song, And those who plundered us requested mirth, Saying, "Sing us one of the songs of Zion!"

(4) How shall we sing the LORD's song In a foreign land?

(5) If I forget you, O Jerusalem, Let my right hand forget its skill!

(6) If I do not remember you, Let my tongue cling to the roof of my mouth— If I do not exalt Jerusalem Above my chief joy.

(7) Remember, O LORD, against the sons of Edom The day of Jerusalem, Who said, "Raze it, raze it, To its very foundation!"

(8) O daughter of Babylon, who are to be destroyed, Happy the one who repays you as you have served us!

(9) Happy the one who takes and dashes Your little ones against the rock! Psa 137:1-9

The setting here is the Babylonian captivity. Judah sat by the rivers of Babylon and wept? Why is this important? It's because their weeping is directly related to their oppression and captivity in Babylon. They wept when they remembered Zion. They were outside of their land. They lived among the oppressor and suffered the trauma of slavery and captivity and the influences of pagan gods. Their spirts were vexed and the practice of their faith was jeopardized and threatened. They were separated from Yahweh's presence and the temple. Thus, they hung their harps on the willows, "weeping willows". Note that Judah's captives required for them a song while they were in a "foreign" land. Judah asked, how can we sing the LORD's song in a foreign land? They could not sing songs of Zion, i.e. songs of praise while they were in captivity. They could only weep and mourn. Rather, they lifted up their voices and wept. As in Egyptian bondage, they groaned and cried while in Babylonian captivity.

Now the above examples were types and shadows of the true bondage of Israel. Jesus spoke to his disciples and told them, that if they continued in His word, they would know the truth and the truth would make them free. The unbelieving Jews responded, "We are Abraham's seed and have never been in bondage to any man". However, the Lord responded that anyone who served sin was the bond slave of sin. They were held in captivity to it, and if they died in their sins, they could not come to the Father. Thus, the bondage of sin was worse, far worse than physical bondage. It stands to reason that if the captivity to sin and death was far worse than the bondage of Egypt and Babylon, then the crying, sorrow, tears and groaning must also be far worse. We submit that the crying and weeping mentioned in Isaiah 65:17, belongs to the "former things" of the old covenant which was a yoke of bondage that could not take away Israel's sins, (Heb. 10:1-4). For those who trusted in Christ, who died for their sins and deliver then out of that ministration of death, they would sing songs of joy with no more crying or weeping. It is all related to the concept of bondage over sin which the physical captivities were the shadows and types.

In Isaiah 25:6-8, the time for singing praises comes when God swallows up death. That is when he would wipe the tears from all faces and remove the rebuke of his people. Notice that this occurs in Yahweh's "holy mountain", which is the kingdom of God, Isaiah 25:6, 2:2-3, 65:25, Dan. 2:44-45. Note the beginning of Isaiah 66:1, "After the time when God brings salvation, (26:9), Isaiah says "In that day this song will be sung in the land of Judah". It means they have been released from bondage, i.e. the bondage of sin and death. The foreign rulers and their dominion ceased (26:12-14). This is Israel's resurrection, their deliverance from oppressors, the greatest of which was the Satan who had the power of death. What is the result? They sing upon coming up out of the land that represents their coming out of the bondage of sin death.

> Your dead shall live; Together with my dead body they shall arise. Awake and sing, you who dwell in dust; For your dew is like the dew of herbs, And the earth shall cast out the dead. Isa 26:19

Observe that upon Judah's resurrection from bondage, they sing. They are freed from bondage. This is the rejoicing spoken of in the new heavens and earth. This is when the weeping and crying ceased. It is the same concept found in Rev. 7:17, 21:4.

Where Righteousness Dwells

The promise of righteousness is the fulfillment of the 70 weeks of Daniel. Since this righteousness is found in the new heavens and earth, it corresponds to the "bringing in of everlasting righteousness spoken of by Daniel.

> "Seventy weeks are determined For your people and for your holy city, To finish the transgression, To make an end of sins, To make reconciliation for iniquity, To bring in everlasting righteousness, To seal up vision and prophecy, And to anoint the Most Holy. Dan 9:24

Daniel says 70 weeks were determined for Judah and for the holy city. This means that within the 70 weeks the holy people and the holy city would be destroyed. See Dan. 12:7, that states when the power of the holy people has been completely shattered, all things would be finished or fulfilled. Therefore, no part of the prophecy can extend beyond the 70 weeks. To finish the transgression refers to Judah filling up their cup of iniquity in murdering the prophets and saints. See Matt. 24:32-38. Israel was charged with murdering the prophets and thus Jesus said he would send to them wise men and scribes, some of whom they would kill and crucify, scourge in their synagogues and persecute from city to city, that upon them would come all the righteous blood shed on the land, from the blood of righteous Abel to the blood of Zechariah son of Berechiah whom they murdered between the temple and the altar. Paul said the Jews filled up their cup in having done these things. They also forbade them to speak to the Gentiles and were contrary to all men.

> For you, brethren, became imitators of the churches of God which are in Judea in Christ Jesus. For you also suffered the same things from your own countrymen, just as they did from the Judeans, (15) who killed both the Lord Jesus and their own prophets, and have persecuted us; and they do not please God and are contrary to all men, (16) forbidding us to speak to the Gentiles that they may be saved, so as always to fill up the measure of their sins; but wrath has come upon them to the uttermost. 1Th 2:14-16

Paul continues the charge against the Judeans for the murder of the prophets and persecution of the saints. As Jesus told them in Matthew 23 to do so, Paul said they were already filling the cup. They had murdered the Lord Jesus, and their own prophets, and persecuted the apostles, did not please God and were contrary to all men. This would bring the wrath of God upon them to the uttermost. John the baptizer spoke of the wrath about to come on the nation of Israel in Matthew 3:7. He said the axe was already laid at the root of the trees and the harvesting fan was in his hands. This indicates that the judgment of God's wrath was already underway. The time of the fulfillment of this wrath is recorded in Revelation chapter 6.

> (12) I looked when He opened the sixth seal, and behold, there was a great earthquake; and the sun became black as sackcloth of hair, and the moon became like blood. (13) And the stars of heaven fell to the earth, as a fig tree drops its late figs when it is shaken by a mighty wind. (14) Then the sky receded as a scroll when it is rolled up, and every mountain and island was moved out of its place. (15) And the kings of the earth, the great men, the rich men, the commanders, the mighty men, every slave and every free man, hid themselves in the caves and in the rocks of the mountains, (16) and said to the mountains and rocks, "Fall on us and hide us from the face of Him who sits on the throne and from the wrath of the Lamb! (17) For the great day of His wrath has come, and who is able to stand?" Rev 6:12-17

Note that this is the time the sun is darkened, become black as sackcloth of hair, and the moon becomes like blood. This is the fulfillment of Joel's prophecy at the great and awesome day of the Lord, (Joel 2:31). It is also quoted in Matthew 24:29, which falls within the scope and historical time frame of the first century generation. The Lord said it could not pass away until all those things were fulfilled. Thus, this darkening of the sun and moon occurred within that generation. Verses 15 and 16 establish this further. John Cites the judgment events of Isaiah 2:10:

> "Enter into the rock, and hide in the dust from the terror of the LORD and the glory of His majesty".

Jesus also refers to the same text and applies it directly to the destruction of Jerusalem.

> But Jesus, turning to them, said, "Daughters of Jerusalem, do not weep for Me, but weep for yourselves and for your children. (29) For indeed the days are coming in which they will say, 'Blessed are the barren, wombs that never bore, and breasts which never nursed!' (30) Then they will begin 'TO SAY TO THE MOUNTAINS, "FALL ON US!" AND TO THE HILLS, "COVER US!" (31) For if they do these things in the green wood, what will be done in the dry?" Luk 23:28-31

Note that he addresses Jerusalem. The "Daughters of Jerusalem" is another way of saying Jerusalem or its people. In the days to come, they would say blessings upon the barren, a condition that normally was cursed in Israel. Pregnancy and childbirth was a blessing and honor. Yet, in the time of their calamity they would say to the mountains, 'Fall on us!' and to the hill, "Cover us!'" This compares precisely with Revelation 6:16, identifying this at the time of God's wrath against Jerusalem, the Mother of Harlots, also called great city of Revelation, spiritually called Sodom and Egypt where the Lord was crucified.

In the book of Revelation when the seventh angel sounds, the angel announces that the nations were angry and the time of God's wrath had come, Rev. 11:15, 18. The wrath is that referred to and spoken of in Matthew 23 and 1 Thessalonians 2:14-16. We say this because it is the time the prophets and the saints were rewarded. In chapter 18 verse 20, the apostles and prophets are avenged on the harlot, Mystery Babylon which is Jerusalem. John quotes from Deuteronomy and says that God had avenged on her the blood of His servants shed by her. (Deut. 32:43; Rev. 19:2) The great city, spiritually called Sodom and Egypt, is the city where also the Lord was crucified. That can be no other city than Jerusalem. Jesus said it cannot be that a prophet perishes outside of Jerusalem. They were ones guilty of charge in the murder of the prophets and saints and of all who were slain in the land. The wrath of God came upon them to the uttermost. Thus the Jews and their holy city Jerusalem and the sanctuary was destroyed within the 70 weeks prophesied by Daniel. The time is well documented in history as 70AD.

It is within this same historical framework of time that God would bring in "everlasting righteousness." This is the promise of the new heaven and new earth because in it righteousness dwells. Paul also quotes from Daniel 9:24, when he spoke of the "hope of righteousness".

> For we through the Spirit eagerly wait for the hope of righteousness by faith. Gal 5:5

When Paul wrote the epistle to the Galatians, he said they were eagerly waiting for the hope of righteousness by faith. Their hope was the new heavens and earth in which righteousness dwells. It was the new covenant, consummated at the wedding and Parousia of Christ. There is a pattern in the teachings of Christ and the apostles that posits the wedding of the Lamb after the destruction of the city. The following chart clearly shows this pattern.

Destruction of the City	The Wedding
Matt. 22:1-7	Matthew 22: 8
Matt. 24	Matt. 25:1-10
Rulers of "this age" Eph. 6:12, Rev. 12:7	Eph. 5:27
Mystery Babylon, Rev. 17:12-19:2	Rev. 19:7,8
Old Jerusalem, Rev. 21:1	Rev. 21:2

The chart therefore shows that the new heavens and earth arrive after the destruction of the city and temple. That means it arrived in 70 AD within the seventy weeks prophesied by Daniel. This being the time of the consummation, (Dan. 9:27) demonstrates that it is the time that vision and prophecy are sealed within those same 70 weeks. It is therefore connected to the end of the people and the sanctuary and destruction of the city, v. 26. The anointing of the most holy is Jesus dedicated the new temple or Most Holy place as we see in Heb. 6:19, 20, 9:24-28. These events were fulfilled in the very, very soon coming of the Lord, per Heb. 10:25, 30, 37.

You Be Diligent to be *Found* in Him

Peter says those in his time who were looking forward to these things, be diligent to be found by Him in peace without spot and blameless. Two important points stand out on this text. The first is the word "found" from "heurisko". This is a technical term for the Parousia. In the judgment of the metallic image dream in Daniel 2, the breaking up of that image results in no trace being *found* after their judgment, Dan. 2:35. Paul, by way of contrast speaks of the faithful and says, he desired to be *found* in Christ, Phil. 3:9. Another occurrence of the word found in Revelation is during the war with Michael and his angels against the dragon.

(7) And war broke out in heaven: Michael and his angels fought with the dragon; and the dragon and his angels fought, (8) but they did not prevail, nor was a place found for them in heaven any longer. Rev 12:7-8

The dragon did not prevail, but was cast out along with his angels, nor was a place found for them anymore. Does anyone doubt that this battle between the dragon, called the "serpent of old, and Satan", refers to the time of the end? One again, this ties in with the 70 weeks of Daniel, and therefore the fall of the city, people and the temple.

Another important fact about this war is that it is directed to the seven churches in Asia, one of which was the church at Ephesus, Rev. 1:4, 11, 20, 2:1-7. Paul described the battle of the church in the Epistle to the Ephesians.

(11) Put on the whole armor of God, that you may be able to stand against the wiles of the devil. (12) For we do not wrestle against flesh and blood, but against principalities, against powers, against the rulers of the darkness of this age, against spiritual hosts of wickedness in the heavenly places. Eph 6:11-12

Observe that the Ephesians had been raised up together with Christ to sit with Him in the heavenlies, (Eph. 1:3, 2:6). Thus, they are the angels waging war with Christ against the dragon. The historical time frame for the war is the age of Moses, called, "this age." In chapter one it stands over against the "age to come" i.e. the age of the full arrival of the new heavens and earth. It was in the age of the old covenant cosmos that the prince of the world, (Eph. 2:2) also called the god of this age (2 Cor. 4:4) operated. Yet, at the end of that age he and his angels were cast out and no place was *found* for them any longer "in heaven."

Further, remember we have developed that Mystery Babylon in Revelation is Jerusalem. This is the great city of Rev. 16:19, that comes up for remembrance before God at the pouring of the bowl (the cup of the wine of the fierceness of God's wrath by the seventh angel. Once this occurred, the same theme is reiterated. "Then every island fled away, and the mountains were not *found.*" And again, in Rev. 20:11 when the first heaven and earth flees from him who sat on the great white throne, the text says "And there was no place *found* for them. This shows the correlation between Dan. 2:35, 2 Pet. 3:14, and Rev. 20:11. That means all these events fall within the 70 weeks of Daniel. The great white throne judgment is thereby established to fall within the historical time of the fall of Jerusalem in 70AD.

The only other writer in the New Testament who uses the word "found" is the Apostle Paul. That is why Peter transitions to the writings of Paul when he speaks of the word "found" and also of being blameless and without spot.

Without Blame and Without Spot

These words are the words refer to the bride who has made herself ready for the marriage. Remember Peter uses the word "hetoimos" twice in 1 Peter 1:5 to speak of the "salvation" that was ready to be revealed in the last time (hour). In chapter four he said God was ready (hetoimos) to judge the living and the dead. The term refers to a bride who has made all the preparations necessary for the wedding which is ready to occur. We have shown that the time of the arrival of the new heavens and new earth is the time the bride descends out of heaven from God, prepared (hetoimos) as a bride adorned for her husband. So the arrival of the new heavens and new earth is the time of the wedding, which follows the destruction of the city of Jerusalem. Isn't it amazing how all this fits as a hand in a glove? The wedding imagery is taken from the Old Testament prophets. In Isaiah 62:1-5, we have the salvation of Zion going forth in brightness as a lamp that burns.

> For Zion's sake I will not hold My peace, And for Jerusalem's sake I will not rest, Until her righteousness goes forth as brightness, And her salvation as a lamp that burns. (2) The Gentiles shall see your righteousness, And all kings your glory. You shall be called by a new name, Which the mouth of the LORD will name. (3) You shall also be a crown of glory In the hand of the LORD, And a royal diadem In the hand of your God. (4) You shall no longer be termed Forsaken, Nor shall your land any more be termed Desolate; But you shall be called Hephzibah, and your land Beulah; For the LORD delights in you, And your land shall be married. (5) For as a young man marries a virgin, So shall

your sons marry you; And as the bridegroom rejoices over the bride, So shall your God rejoice over you. Isa 62:1-5

The lamp suggests oil the virgins of Matthew 15:1-10 carried in their lamps in preparation for the wedding. The bride would no longer be forsaken by crowned with glory and married. They salvation arrives at the Parousia of Christ, Isaiah 62:11, 12. It is the time of the making of the new covenant mentioned in Hosea 2:16-23. This is when the Gentiles would see the righteousness of God, and all the kings His glory.

"And it shall be, in that day," Says the LORD, "That you will call Me 'My Husband,' And no longer call Me 'My Master,' [17] For I will take from her mouth the names of the Baals, And they shall be remembered by their name no more. [18] In that day I will make a covenant for them With the beasts of the field, With the birds of the air, And with the creeping things of the ground. Bow and sword of battle I will shatter from the earth, To make them lie down safely. [19] "I will betroth you to Me forever; Yes, I will betroth you to Me In righteousness and justice, In lovingkindness and mercy; [20] I will betroth you to Me in faithfulness, And you shall know the LORD. [21] "It shall come to pass in that day That I will answer," says the LORD; "I will answer the heavens, And they shall answer the earth. [22] The earth shall answer With grain, With new wine, And with oil; They shall answer Jezreel. [23] Then I will sow her for Myself in the earth, And I will have mercy on her who had not obtained mercy; Then I will say to those who were not My people, 'You are My people!' And they shall say, 'You are my God!'" Hos 2:16-23

Paul said the bride would be without spot or wrinkle. Peter is using the marriage language from Paul's eschatological teaching to speak of the time when the church is found in Christ as a chaste virgin without spot and blameless. Eph. 5:27.

Paul's Writings Hard to Be Understood

Aside from John in the book of Revelation, Paul uses more of the O.T. imagery in His writings coupled with sharp reasoning and logic than almost any other writing. Many have tried to understand him from a Greek or Western oriented mindset. This results in utter confusion and failure. Confusion is one of the most often expressed terms by those who seek to interpret all things eschatology in a very naturalistic and materialistic fashion. When they hear the spiritual application of many of these things, they say, "I'm confused." The confusion is not with the text or the Scriptures, but with their approach to the word of God. Peter says Paul wrote many things that were hard to be understood, but not impossible to understand. It is the untaught and unstable who twist Paul's and Peter's teaching on eschatology. Those in the first century did so unto their own destruction. However, when we allow the words of the Prophets to guide our interpretation, we more easily see the truth of these matters. Paul said, he was given revelations in the mystery of God, by which when we read, we would understand his knowledge in the mystery of Christ, (Eph. 3:3-4).

Summary

We demonstrated that the term "earth" as translated from the Hebrew eretz means land our country usually referring to Palestine, but also to other regions, such as Egypt or Babylon, etc. This term is used thousands of times in this manner. That however does not restrict its use in a global sense in passages where the context clearly indicates such usages. We systematically addressed the arguments that were believed to support a yet future universal coming of the Lord after 70AD by investigating all the earth in context.

We demonstrated that the "day and hour" of Matthew 24:36, and its correspondent text of unexpectedness in Luke 21:33, does not refer to a future coming of the Lord. The Old Testament prophecies in Deuteronomy 32:29, 35 and Zechariah 14:6 prophesied of a day sealed in God's treasures and was known only to the Lord. Both texts prophesy of the destruction of Jerusalem and the end of the Old Covenant people in A.D. 70.

We also demonstrated that while Moses named the precise "crooked and perverse generation," he never names the day and hour. Thus, it is possible to know the generation, but not the precise day and hour. Secondly, we demonstrated that the judgment upon all the earth could not mean a future destruction of the universe. The lexical use of these terms shows conclusively that they all mean the same event and time, i.e. the fall of Jerusalem in A.D. 70.

The whole inhabited earth of Matthew 24:14, equals the inhabited earth of Luke 21:26. But whole earth of Mathew 24:14, also equaled all the earth of Romans 10:18 and the whole inhabited earth of Revelation 3:10. We then showed that Revelation 3:10, Matthew 24:14

and Luke 24:14 and Luke 21:26 harmoniously pointed to A.D. 70 whether "all" is included or omitted.

Thirdly, Paul's hermeneutic or method of interpretation was the Law and the Prophets. His eschatology drew from and found its fulfillment in the last days of the Old Covenant Jewish age.

Next, we showed the fallacy of the attempt to divide Luke 21:33 and its parallel text in Matthew 24:36. The context of the judgments upon Noah and Lot's generations respectively with the texts in Deuteronomy forever puts that idea to rest.

We demonstrated that God knows how to communicate the times in which his judgments and blessings occur. He knew how to tell Abraham he would die before the fulfillment of the promise in the fourth generation. He knew how to tell Daniel that he would rest until the time of the end. He also knew to tell Peter and his hearers that those things spoken by the prophets would come upon them before their generation died! Thus, Luke 21:34-35, showed no distinction in the audience separated by many generations, but belonged exclusively to the generation addressed in the first century by Jesus and later in the apostolic writings.

Finally, we presented a verse by verse break down of 2 Peter 3 showing how it was fulfilled in AD 70.

Addendum

Due to the influence and polemic discussions surrounding Tim Martin and Jeffrey Vaughn's well received *Beyond Creation Science* book, I have chosen to append the following in response to some of the premises in their writings which provide opportunity for study:

The Host of Heaven

According to Martin and Vaughn, the term "host of heaven" in Genesis 2:1, refers to Covenant Creation versus Cosmic Creation. Support is cited in Exodus 12:51 where the same Hebrew word is used in Genesis. References are also cited from Daniel 8:10-13, 19.

BCS authors write. "The subject of the creation account is the "host"—God's army—which is a new people. Genesis 2:4 (KJV) offers another indicator: "These are the generations of the heavens and of the earth when they were created, in the day that the Lord God made the earth and the heavens."

Further they ask, "Why is it that the "heavens and earth" involve generations? The form of this verse ("These are the generations of...") is used through Genesis e.g., 5:1; 6:9; 10:1, 32; 11:10). In every other instance where the form is used, the reference is to people. Genesis 2:4 references generations in conjunction with "heaven and earth" because the creation account speaks about the original formation of God's people.[24] From this, they conclude that the Genesis statement is symbolic repre-

---

[24] Fulfilled Magazine, Winter 2008, Vol. 3, Issue 4, Perspectives, Timothy P. Martin, Jeffrey L. Vaughn, ed. Brian L. Martin, p. 11-12.

sentative of real people in real history describing the beginning of God's covenant world of friendship and relationship with his people.

But, can this claim that "host" in Genesis be made as symbolic and as an exclusive reference to people? Let's cite the same author of Genesis in his message to Israel in Deuteronomy chapter 5. According to the LXX (Septuagint—Greek translation of the Old Testament), "host" is rendered cosmos in Gen. 2:1.

First observe that God "declared to you [Israel] His covenant which He Command you to perform, the Ten Commandments; and He wrote them on two tablets of stone. God specially warns Israel that at that time he called them to be nation and gave them to the law, that they saw no form, carved imaged or figure. Then he says the following:

"And take heed, lest you lift your eyes to heaven, and when you see the sun, the moon, and the stars, all the host of heaven, you feel driven to worship them and serve them, which the Lord your God has given to all the peoples under the whole heaven as a heritage. But the Lord has taken you and brought you out of the iron furnace, out of Egypt, to be His people, an inheritance, as you are this day," Deut. 4:19-20).

That the reference is to the material creation cannot be doubted as God speaks of male or female, birds of the air, creeping things on the ground and fish in the waters beneath the earth. (16-18) Now, when Israel looks up toward the heavens, do they see Adam and Eve in a covenant relationship with God? Do they see people living in the heavens? Do we not have the very phrase, "host of heaven" used with the identical creation language of Genesis 1 and 2, speaking of the material creation—a creation Israel was forbidden to worship or to make any likeness or in the form of a carved imaged?

The gods Moses warned against were the very God's that Egypt worshiped. The Egyptians did not worship the God of heaven under Pharaoh but gods of the sun, moon, stars and four-footed beasts, the Nile River and those things in the sea. In Exodus 32, Israel asked for gods like those of Egypt, and Aaron acquiesced in forming a graven image of the golden calf. "They have turned aside quickly out of the way which I commanded them. They have made themselves a molded calf, and worshiped it and sacrificed to it, and said, "This is your god, O Israel, that brought you out of the land of Egypt." (Ex. 32:8)

Was the covenant that God gave to all peoples under the whole heaven as a heritage a covenant of people? Is not God speaking of the material heavens and earth which have been given to all peoples under the heavens as an eternal heritage? Did He not promise that in Genesis 8:21-22 in the covenant made with Noah?

Again, in Deut. 17:2-5, God warns Israel against worshiping the "creation," versus the "Creator". "If there is found among you, within any of your gages which the Lord your God gives you, a man or a woman who has been wicked in the sight of the Lord your God, in transgressing His covenant, who has gone and served other gods and worshiped them, either the sun or moon or any of the host of heaven, which I have not commanded, and it is told you, and you hear of it, then you shall inquire diligently. And if it is indeed true and certain that such an abomination has been committed in Israel, then you shall bring out to your gages that man or woman who has committed that wicked thing, and shall stone to death that man or woman with stones." (my emp. WHB)

The word 'host' is Strong's number "6635" in both Genesis and the texts cited.[25] Now Israel (the Northern tribes) violated God's law and did exactly what he warned them not to do. They worshiped the **host of heaven** and made for themselves carved images. "…they followed idols, became idolaters, and went after the nations who were all around them, concerning whom the Lord had charged them that they should not do like them. So they left all the commandments of the Lord their God, made for themselves a molded image and two calves, made a wooden image and worshiped all the **host of heaven**, and served Baal." (2 Ki. 17:15-16) See additional references to Israel's idolatry in worshiping the "host of heaven" 2 Kings 21:3, 5; 23:4, 5; 2 Chron. 33:3,5.

---

[25] James H. Strong, Strong's Exhaustive Concordance of the Bible, p. 492

Daniel 8:10-13

The attempt to support the arguments using Daniel appears to be an example of circular reasoning. This is what strikes me odd in the Covenant Creation paradigm. This is not to say that I don't agree with much of what Martin and Vaughn brought to the table in terms of research. But, I think their biggest sell is yet to be convincing at least to me. As a Preterist, and as they acknowledge, the conclusions reached are contingent upon context, namely time statements which preclude the literal use of the terms. However, in establishing context for Covenant Creation, where are the temporal conditions for reinterpreting the language to refer to covenant versus cosmic?

It is not enough in my judgment to say that Genesis or Daniel refers to instances where the "host of heaven" means people. The issue is that of establishing the law of type and antitype, of literal and figurative language. The rules of language appear to imply to imply that the literal gives birth to the figurative and not the opposite way round. In every case the references cited assume or argue that Genesis 1:1f is figurative. From this, proof is sought in passages written later to support that premise. On the other hand, with types, and antitypes, shadows and realities, the origin is established first, then the figurative language draws from it. Else, how do we establish the basic meaning of anything?

Let me try to illustrate further. If the first mention of animals is people, where do we find a reference to establish that an animal? What determines the figurative use? If a giraffe or elephant is some type of giant human Nephilim, when and how are we to come to understand that a giraffe is a giraffe or an elephant is an elephant? The same is true for a "beginning" and a "heaven and earth." If beginning means that of a covenant people where is the prototype for understanding what a beginning means? If heaven and earth is covenant in first mention, then when did it come to mean the physical creation?

Is it reasonable to go back and say the figurative use of heaven and earth determines the physical use of the terms? Did God make a covenant people before he had a physical world and provisions in which to sustain them? How much good would that have been to a covenant people dependent upon physical sustenance to survive?

How does one come to know what the "tree of life" and the "tree of knowledge of good and evil is," apart from knowing what a "tree" is? Do the latter establish the meaning of a tree first before we can have a tree? What about the earth, the grass, [Botanen, or botany] fruit trees producing fruit *after its kind*, (Gen. 1:11-12). Do all of these have a covenant meaning that is later revealed to mean a literal botanic kingdom? Therefore, it is suspect to use Daniel to establish the meaning of "host of heaven" in Genesis simply because the same phraseology is there. What about the references cited from Deut. 17:3 and 2 Ki. 17:15-16? Daniel is admittedly speaking in highly symbolic terms and apocalyptic imagery. L

> "And it grew up to the host of heaven; and it cast down some of the host and some of the stars to the ground, and trampled them. He even exalted himself as high as the Prince of the host; and by him the daily sacrifices were taken away, and the places of His sanctuary was cast down. Because of transgression, an army was given over to the horn to oppose the daily sacrifices; and he cast truth down to the ground. He did all this and prospered. Then I heard a holy one speaking; and another holy one said to the certain one who was speaking, "how long will the vision be, concerning the daily sacrifices and the transgression of desolation, the giving of both the sanctuary and the host to be trampled underfoot." (Dan. 8:10-13)

Now, the response to this is the enigmatic 2,300 days. Gabriel interprets the vision for Daniel saying that it refers to the time of the end, (8:17). Thus, he was to seal up the vision for it refers to many days in the future." (Dan. 8:26) Since this vision referred to "the" time of "the" end, I take it to refer to the A.D. 70 casting down of the Old Covenant people of Israel, particularly Judah. Its counterpart is seen in Revelation 12:4, where a third of the stars are thrown down to the earth in defeat.

Generation in Genesis

Generation from "geneseos", (geneseos, genitive singular of genesis) used in Gen. 2:4, is offered as proof that God speaks of the covenant world versus the material creation. However, the word may include the creation of man but also include all species of animals and plants that beget or generate through procreation. Why limit this term to mankind or covenant in this context? Both plants and animals are likewise capable of generation offspring are they not? The tables below are from J.B. Smith's Greek Concordance.[26]

1078. Genesis

Book	Oc.	Generation	Oc.	Natural	Oc.	Nature	Total
Mt.	1	1:1					1
Jas.			1	1:23	1	3.6	2
Total	1		1		1		3

Note that the term genesis (Strong's 1078), refers both to humankind and nature. Matthew speaks of the generations (genesis) of Jesus Christ. Moulton includes James' reference in 1:23. He defines genesis to mean birth nativity, Matt. 1;18; Lu. 1:14; Ja. 1:23; successive generation, descent, lineage, Matt. 1:1...."[27]

In Matthew 3:7, John, the Baptist calls Judah a "generation" of vipers. The word used is gennema (gennema, Strong's #1081), and means what is born or produced, Matt. 26:29; 14:25; offspring, progeny, brood, Matt. 3:7; 12:34; fruit, produce, fruit, increase, Lu. 12:18; 2 Cor. 9:10. J.B. Smith, shows that the word is also used to refer to the generation or procreation of fruit. [28]

[26] J.B. Greek-English Concordance To The New Testament, © 1955, p. 70, Mennonite Publishing House.
[27] Samuel Moulton, The Analytical Greek Lexicon Revised 1978 Edition, p. 79, The Zondervan Corporation.
[28] Ibid, p. 70.

1081. gennema

Book	Oc.	Fruit	Oc.	Generation	Total
Mt.	1	26:29	3	3:7; 12:34; 23:33	4
Mk.	1	14:25			1
Lk.	2	12:18; 22:18	1	3:7	3
2 Co.	1				1
Total	5	9:10	4		9

While the term is admittedly used figuratively, it nonetheless shows that Smith used gennema (Strong's 1081) to refer to the plant and animal kingdoms. However, this may not be totally accurate. A kindred word genema—observe the variant spelling) means offspring, by analogy to produce literally or figuratively. Moulton gives references from Luke 12:18; 2 Cor. 9:10, rendering it natural produce, fruit, increase implying the fruit of the ground.[29]

The Vocabulary of the Greek Testament concurs with this observation. "The spelling genema, "fruit of the earth," shown in the best MSS (manuscripts) in Mt. 26:29, Mk. 14:25, etc., is now abundantly attested from the papyri…(A.D. 197)…inscription from Egypt (A.D. 68)…and Syria (iii/AD). On the phrase on ostraca of the imperial period genematos tou deinos etous, referring to the duty payable on the harvest of the preceding year…hence the world genematograpeein, "confiscate by the government". They also cite "produce and surplus produce." The distinction between gennema and genema is that the former refers to animals while the latter refers to plants.

"The history of this word, unknown to LS, and unsuspected except as a blunder of NT uncials, is peculiarly instructive. Against HR, who regard the totally distinct words gennema and genema as mere variants of spelling, Thackery (Gr. i.p. 118) shows that gennema (from gennao)

---

[29] Ibid, p. 79.

is LXX *animal*, and genema vegetable, as in NT. The hundreds of instances quotable from Egypt must not close our eyes to the apparent absence of attestation elsewhere, except in Syria, which accounts for its appearance in NT when gennemata = "vegetable produce" we should drop the second "n". This is confirmed by the strictures of Phrynichus (Lobeck, p. 286).[30] In the Lucan passage, the reference to vegetable produce is unmistakable.

"So he said, 'I will do this: I will pull down my barns [granaries] and build greater, and there I will store all my crops [produce, ta genemata] and my goods." (Luke 12:18). A figurative use of the word is found in 2 Cor. 9:10: "Now may He who supplies seed to the sower, and bread for food, supply and multiply the seed you have sown and increase the fruits [gennemata] of your righteousness," Note the blunder the translators make with the spelling in light of Moulton and Milligan's research. The reference here is obviously that of produce or vegetables and should correctly be rendered genemata with one "n" as in Luke 12:18.

Since God speaks of the "host of heaven" to refer to the creation in Genesis 1-2, and the likeness of the birds, beasts, fish, humans and the heavenly bodies of the sun, moon and starts, then is it not reasonable to understand that he used "generations" in regard to these? In Nehemiah 9:6, we find God saying that all the "host heaven" worships Him

"You alone are the Lord; You have made heaven, the heaven of heavens, with all their host, the earth and everything on it, the seas and all that is in them, and you preserve them all. The host of heaven worships you."

This reflects the doxology of the 148th Psalm where everything God created praises Him. Angels, hosts, sea creatures, elements, bird's plants, beasts and mankind join together in praising their Creator. Observe that immediately after mentioning the hosts, God says the sun, moon stars and heaven of heavens and waters above the heavens. Surely "host of heaven" can by no stretch of the imagination refer only to the creation of a covenant people in this text. The focus here is the material non-covenantal creation. Nor can "generation" be limited to people but

---

[30] James Hope Moulton, and George Milligan, The Vocabulary of the Greek Testament Illustrated from the Papyri and Other Non-Literary Sources, © 1930, Eerdman's p. 123.

includes the material creation as well per Genesis 2:4. God says let everything that has breath praise Him, Psa. 150:6.

The Heavens and the Earth

Martin and Vaughn make the point that Joseph's dream uses symbolic imagery of heaven and earth.

"We see the association of all three symbolic elements of creation in the promise given to Abraham (Gen. 13:16; 15:4-6; 22:17) and also in Joseph's dream, Gen. 37:6-11)." Our question is, where in Genesis does God speak of the literal creation of heaven if not in chapter one? If He does, how do we know that it's not symbolism? How do we know that it is? When God told Abraham that his seed would be innumerable as the sand on the seashore and the stars of heaven is God reasoning from symbolism? In other words, do signs *sign-i-fy* themselves?

It seems reasonable that if anyone has stepped onto a beach, the mind cannot begin to grasp the vast amount of granules on the beach as far as one can see. This to me provides a most excellent and reasonable context for such a statement as an innumerable seed to fulfill the promise. However, if God is referring to figurative sand and stars, then it does not seem reasonable. Again, it seems to me that the major issues here is that of starting from a symbolical referent, i.e. an antitype to reason back to the type, to move from the reality to the shadow. The text cited in Deuteronomy 32:1 unquestionably depicts Israel as the covenantal heaven and earth. God has just "formed" Israel as a covenant people in Sinai. This is their beginning.

That God uses "creation language" proves that the actual creation is the genre of language for such reference. The reference in verse one should be interpreted in the light of Deut. 4:26. There, God calls heaven and earth to witness against Israel, that they will perish off the land if they or their grandchildren corrupt themselves with idolatry.

In Deuteronomy 32:10-11, the writers acknowledge that God found Israel in a desert land and in the wasteland, a howling wilderness; at which time he encircled him, instructed him (gave him the law) and kept him as the apple of His eye. God's protective care is as an eagle hovering over its young, spreading out its wings taking them up and carrying them on its wings. This was Israel's beginning when there was no foreign God in him.

In other words, at the giving of the Law in Sinai (when God purged them from their sins with the golden calf, Israel was born of God, nursed and brought out of the wilderness into Canaan. That is her beginning. Jeremiah 31:31-32, Heb. 8:7-8, both speak of the covenant which God made with Israel when he took them by the hand to lead them out of the land of Egypt. When God spoke with Abraham, he told the patriarch he would deliver his seed after 400 years, (Gen. 15:13). Paul, quoting the text says, the Law (Old Covenant) came 430 years after the promise made to Abraham, (Gal. 3:19). Thus, we have the time of the beginning of Israel's covenant. To say that the words "waste" and "however" occur only one other time, in Genesis 1, does not prove that they are figurative. Rather, it shows the precedent for showing that "waste" and "hover" are used when God forms a new creation.

There is no question that the Spirit of God was "hovering" over the church until Christ was "formed in you" as Paul figuratively travailed in birth. This was the time of God's new creation in Christ. It does not mean the church was created in Genesis 1.

Ezekiel 16 describes Israel as a newborn castaway in the wilderness. Dying and writhing in its own blood with its navel uncut God nourished up as a plant until it grew and matured. God courted her, loved her and entered into a covenant. Note how she is clothed with the imagery of the tabernacle. This again points to the wilderness. It is the time Israel is "without form and void" until God hovers over her to form her into his bride.

Martin and Vaughn write: "If the revelation of the Sinai covenant could recreate and reorganize the world, then the world in focus as God's creation could not be the physical universe." Fulfilled, p. 13. We agree. These words properly belong to Israel and her Old Covenant. Further, we readily accept all the imagery of the tabernacle typology in Genesis. That is not the point.

The language here and in Jeremiah 4:23-29, is clearly the destruction, the returning to "nothing" or a "waste and barren" land after the invasion of the Chaldeans. It is the context which provides the meaning and application of the "waste and barren" land. The precedent for that language is Gen. 1:1-2. The context determines the application. Otherwise, there would be no way to determine whether it is literal or figurative.

Again, the language is similar to that Genesis. However, the condition of Adam is carried forward through the Mosaic covenant in dealing with the problem of sin and death. Israel's return to a "waste and barren" land is the language of covenantal curses. It stands in juxtaposition to a land flowing with milk and honey.

Creation in Genesis Chapter 1

Martin and Vaughn seek to establish the premise that the creation of Genesis 1 is covenantal versus cosmic. They cite 2 Cor. 4:6 and Heb. 1:10-11. We have already commented on the latter text above. Concerning the former, there is nothing in the text that would not apply or be valid as a reference to the material creation. It is a simple declaration. For it is the God who commanded light to shine out of darkness, who has shown in our hearts to give the light of the knowledge of the glory of God in the face of Jesus Christ."

Understanding physical light allows one to understand the meaning of light in this text. Consider a similar expression in Acts 17:24-28. God, who made the world and everything in it, since He is Lord of heaven and earth, does not dwell in temples made with hands. Nor is He worshiped with men's hands, as through He needed anything, since He gives to all life, breath, and all things. "And He has made from one blood every nation of men to dwell on all the face of the earth, and has determined their preappointed times and the boundaries of their dwellings, so that they should seek the Lord, in the hope that they might grope for Him and find Him, through He is not far from each one of us; for in Him we live and move and have our being, as also some of your own poets have said, "For we are also His offspring."

This text refers to the creation, not of Israel, but of all men. It says God made the world and everything in it and He is Lord of heaven and earth. Is this covenant creation? Were the bounds of men's habitation only within the covenant God made with Israel? Next these writers cite 2 Peter 3:5-7, to justify a covenant creation. But they inconsistently claim that God uses the creation of Genesis 1 to destroy the creation of Noah. Here is what we mean. Martin and Vaughn acknowledge that the heavens were of old and the earth stood out of the water and in the water. Then they agree that the people of Noah's day perished being flood with water, i.e. by the creation of Genesis 1!

That can only mean that if Genesis 1 is covenant creation, i.e. of Israel, then God uses Israel, the covenant people to destroy the people in Noah's day. Thus, the flood was simply the covenant people of God. That is the logic of Martin and Vaughn. It does not appear to be very logical. Martin and Vaughn abandon their premise totally a Second Peter 3. They attempt to demonstrate from Revelation 21:1 that the old heaven and earth and the sea are covenantal and end in A.D. 70. We agree however, they imposed that meaning on Genesis 1, to which we do not agree for the reasons above.

Again, if the heavens and earth of Revelation 21:1, equals that of Genesis 1, then the covenant people are the flood or the flood is the result of the breaking up of the covenant people, i.e. heavens and earth. Further, they make an analogy between the flood of Noah's day and the "fire" of the apostolic era in its destruction of the existing heaven and earth, i.e. the old covenant Israel. What can this mean? If logic serves me, it means that the covenant people are both the water and the fire!

Now let us draw the logical conclusion of that premise. If the flood and fire are equivalent and as we have demonstrated that their logic demands that the waters of the flood are the covenant people of Genesis 1, then likewise the "fire" must be the covenant people of Genesis 1. This bring us to the conclusion that the covenant people are the fire which destroys the covenant people in 2 Peter 3:5-7. Therefore, according to Martin and Vaughn, the Israel, the covenant people, destroy Israel, the covenant people in 2 Peter 3.

This we believe is the inconsistency and illogical conclusion of citing Genesis 1 as a covenantal versus material creation. We thank Martin and Vaughn for raising the questions, but we feel they have not adequately worked through the logic of their covenantal premise. I believe that it is being weighed in the balances and found wanting.

Bibliography

Curtis Cates, The A.D. 70 Theology

Timothy P. Martin and Jeffrey L. Vaughn, Beyond Creation Science, Covenant Creation from Genesis to Revelation

William Bell, Jr, The Re-Examination, A Review of William Jones' An Examination of the A.D. 70 Teaching,

Drew Leonard, The A.D. 70 Teaching, End of Time Southaven 2017 Lectures, Southaven Church of Christ, Southaven

Guy N. Woods, A Commentary on the Second Epistle of Peter

Ted J. Clark
http://www.kccofc.org/39th/Lectures/2000%20Manuscripts/-Clarke%20-%20AD%2070.PDF

Mark Biltz, Blood Moons: Decoding the Imminent Heavenly Signs

D. R Dungan, Hermeneutics, p. 270

John A.T. Robertson, Word Pictures of the New Testament, Broadman Press

Ethelbert W. Bullinger, Figures of Speech Uses in the Bible

Edward Young, The New International Commentary on the Old Testament, The Book of Isaiah Vol. I

The Last Days Identified, by Don K. Preston with Contributions by John Anderson

English Version of the Bible with the corresponding Greek words in line with the English.

New International Commentary of the New Testament

Flavius Josephus, Antiquities of the Jews, Bk. 3.6.4

Philo, XVII

NICNT, e-Sword Version

James H. Strong, Strong's Exhaustive Concordance of the Bible

J.B. Greek-English Concordance To The New Testament, © 1955, p. 70, Mennonite Publishing House

Samuel Moulton, The Analytical Greek Lexicon Revised 1978 Edition, p. 79, The Zondervan Corporation.

James Hope Moulton, and George Milligan, The Vocabulary of the Greek Testament Illustrated from the Papyri and Other Non-Literary Sources, © 1930

Other books by William Bell

Living in Eternity: Christ In You, The Realized Hope of Glory

The 23rd Psalm: The Good Shepard in the Temple of God

Ship-Wrecked Faith: Trans-Atlantic Slave Trade or A.D. 70?

The Re-Examination- A Review of William Jones' "And Examination of the A.D. 70 Teaching"

DVD Series:
"The Last Days" 5 DVD's Plus 1 PowerPoint CD for Each Lesson

YouTube Channel: William Bell-AllThingsFulfilled

Website: AllThingsFulfilled.com

Made in the USA
Monee, IL
04 June 2023

35000489R00085